WE LOVE COLOR

16 Iconic Quilt Designers Create with Kona® Solids

Compiled by Susanne Woods

stash BOOKS®

an imprint of C&T Publishing

Text, Photography, and Artwork copyright © 2012 by C&T Publishing, Inc.

Publisher: Amy Marson

Creative Director: Gailen Runge

Editor: Cynthia Bix

Technical Editors:
Ann Haley and Teresa Stroin

Cover/Book Designer:
Kristy Zacharias

Page Layout Artist: Kerry Graham

Production Coordinator:
Jessica Jenkins

Production Editor: S. Michele Fry

Illustrator: Tim Manibusan

Photography by Christina Carty-Francis and Diane Pedersen of C&T Publishing, Inc., unless otherwise noted

Published by Stash Books, an imprint of C&T Publishing, Inc., P.O. Box 1456, Lafayette, CA 94549.

Library of Congress Cataloging-in-Publication Data

We love color : 16 iconic quilt designers create with Kona solids / compiled by Susanne Woods.

 p. cm.

ISBN 978-1-60705-544-0 (soft cover)

1. Quilting. 2. Colors. I. Woods, Susanne.

TT835.W386 2012

746.46--dc23

2011040136

Printed in China

10 9 8 7 6 5 4 3 2 1

CONTENTS

NOTE

All fabrics called for in the projects in this book are Kaufman Kona Cotton Solids, available at quilting and fabric stores, or visit robertkaufman.com (for wholesale inquiries or where-to-buy information). These fabrics are 44˝ wide. For a complete list of all the colors used in the book, see Resources (page 146).

INTRODUCTION

The Kona story began some 30 years ago, at a time when Robert Kaufman Company was focused primarily on making apparel fabrics for the home sewer. Little did we know that introducing our new Kona Cotton Solids would mark the beginnings of what would become the industry mainstay for quilting solids. Today, Robert Kaufman Company produces and ships millions of yards of Kona internationally and throughout the United States every year, and the Kona brand has become synonymous with the idea of a quality quilting solid.

So what's the Kona difference?

It is frequently said that Kona is a 60″ × 60″ square cotton sheeting—a basic cotton cloth that is woven and sourced all over the world. But that hides the whole truth. Mills using these stocks rarely produce a quality that meets our standards. Producing a quality solid is actually more difficult than producing a print. Solids reveal all the flaws that can easily be hidden in a printed fabric. For this reason, Robert Kaufman Company specially produces its own goods rather than using stock quality. The yarns used in Kona are cleaned before weaving to eliminate excessive slubs and cottonseed, and then extra yarn is added to the construction to bulk up the goods. The result is a smooth, even finish and Kona's signature bulky hand. Additionally, all Kona is certified to meet the Oeko-Tex standard for no hazardous chemicals.

With more than 200 colors in the Kona range, the brand presents countless possibilities for home sewing enthusiasts and quiltmakers of all skill levels. Solids are timely as well as utterly timeless. From traditional Amish quilts to the most modern graphic quilt, solids speak to both traditionalist quiltmakers and to the new generation of sewers who represent the modern quilting movement.

To celebrate the creative spirit and the endless inspiration of Kona Cotton Solids, we have partnered with some of the modern quilt movement's leading designers to compile in this book 16 fresh, exciting quilt projects made exclusively with Kona Cotton Solids. The following pages are sure to inspire your inner quilt artist. So break out your Kona Cotton Color Card, choose from its many enticing colors, and create!

Happy sewing!

HARVEY KAUFMAN
Robert Kaufman Company

CENTERED

Designed and made by Cherri House and machine quilted by Angela Walters

This quilt symbolizes a turning point in my life. When, at 32, I found myself a single mother of four young children, it quickly became apparent that it was going to take all that I had, and more, to not fail at the task. Between working and trying to raise my children, life was as hectic as could be. My faith—always a guiding light in my life—became more important than ever before. I pleaded for guidance, and the answer I received was, "Be the mother." I interpreted this to mean that instead of being scattered, my children and I needed to be centered—to be one in purpose and to make our family and each other our first priority. Being centered enabled me to raise my family, to keep my priorities straight, and to give my children the counsel they needed to conduct their own lives.

This quilt represents that time—the very core of being solid and steadfast, and the light and illumination that being centered brought into my life and the lives of my children. Though simple in design, this large Courthouse Steps pattern becomes a study in color, and the piecing is a vehicle to achieve the end result. The graduated hues radiate from a center core into a burst of light, bright color.

MATERIALS AND SUPPLIES

Black, **Indigo**, **Navy**, **Windsor**: ⅛ yard each

Cadet, **Delft**, **Denim**, **Candy Blue**, Blueberry, Lake, Cloud, **Blue**, Sky, Mint: ⅓ yard each

Honey Dew, Pear, **Sour Apple**: ⅜ yard each

Kiwi, **Clover**, **Holly**, **Kelly**: ½ yard each

Spruce: ½ yard for binding

Backing: 4 yards

Batting: 70″ × 70″

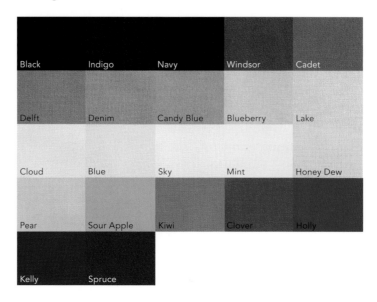

CUTTING

From the Black fabric, cut 1 square 2½″ × 2½″ for the quilt center.

From the Spruce fabric, cut 7 strips 2″ × width of fabric (WOF) for binding.

For the rest of the fabrics, refer to the chart to cut the number of WOF strips indicated for each color. Subcut these strips as indicated in the two right columns. You will need to sew some WOF strips together before you can subcut them.

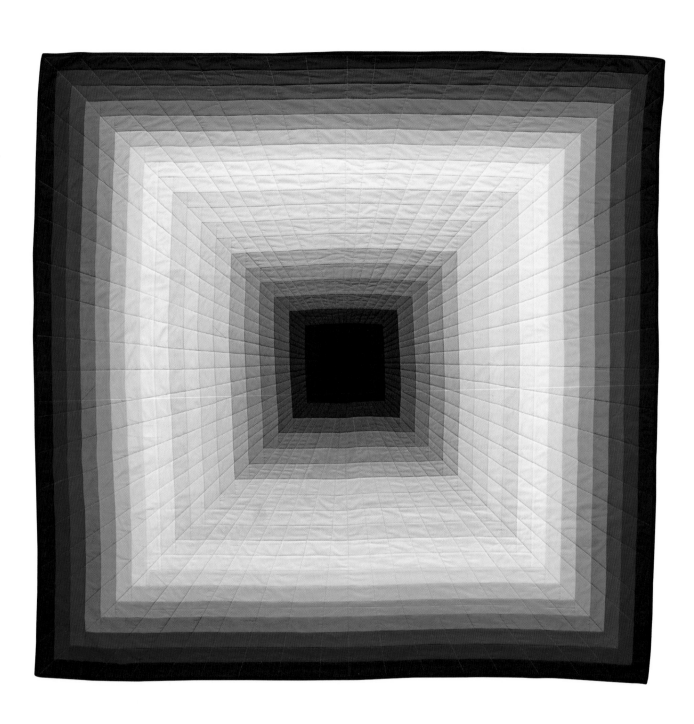

FABRIC	COLOR	NUMBER OF STRIPS CUT 2″ × WOF	JOIN STRIPS?	A: SUBCUT 2 @	B: SUBCUT 2 @
2	Indigo	1		2″ × 2½″	2″ × 5½″
3	Navy	1		2″ × 5½″	2″ × 8½″
4	Windsor	1		2″ × 8½″	2″ × 11½″
5	Cadet	2		2″ × 11½″	2″ × 14½″
6	Delft	2		2″ × 14½″	2″ × 17½″
7	Denim	2		2″ × 17½″	2″ × 20½″
8	Candy Blue	3	X	2″ × 20½″	2″ × 23½″
9	Blueberry	3	X	2″ × 23½″	2″ × 26½″
10	Lake	3	X	2″ × 26½″	2″ × 29½″
11	Cloud	4		2″ × 29½″	2″ × 32½″
12	Blue	4		2″ × 32½″	2″ × 35½″
13	Sky	4		2″ × 35½″	2″ × 38½″
14	Mint	4		2″ × 38½″	2″ × 41½″
15	Honey Dew	5	X	2″ × 41½″	2″ × 44½″
16	Pear	5	X	2″ × 44½″	2″ × 47½″
17	Sour Apple	5	X	2″ × 47½″	2″ × 50½″
18	Kiwi	6	X	2″ × 50½″	2″ × 53½″
19	Clover	6	X	2″ × 53½″	2″ × 56½″
20	Holly	6	X	2″ × 56½″	2″ × 59½″
21	Kelly	7	X	2″ × 59½″	2″ × 62½″

INSTRUCTIONS

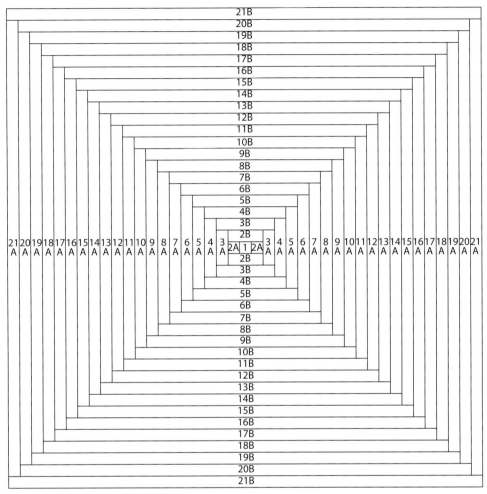

Quilt assembly diagram

To help construction go smoothly and keep everything in order, create small labels for colors 2 through 21, and attach them to the corresponding cut pieces. Refer to the assembly diagram to lay out the pieces in the order in which they will be sewn (2 through 21).

Quilt top assembly

This quilt is constructed like a large Courthouse Steps block. As you sew, press the seam allowances away from the center with each new fabric piece added.

1. Sew a 2″ × 2½″ Indigo piece (2A) to the left and right sides of the Black square.

2. Sew the 2″ × 5½″ Indigo pieces (2B) to the top and bottom of the unit from Step 1.

3. Sew the 2″ × 5½″ Navy pieces (3A) to the left and right sides of the unit from Step 2.

4. Sew the 2″ × 8½″ Navy pieces (3B) to the top and bottom of the unit from Step 3.

5. Continue this sequence with all the remaining color pieces.

NOTE

To keep the quilt top flat and prevent curves as you sew, pin the strips, beginning at approximately Fabric 8 (Candy Blue), before sewing.

Quilting and finishing

1. Mark your quilting design on the quilt top, or plan to quilt without marking.

2. Use your favorite method or refer to Quiltmaking Basics (page 135) to layer and baste the quilt top, batting, and backing.

3. Quilt as desired. The stitching on my quilt—straight lines radiating out to the edges from the center—is very simple yet emphasizes the movement of the design.

4. Refer to Quiltmaking Basics or use your preferred method to bind the quilt using the Spruce strips.

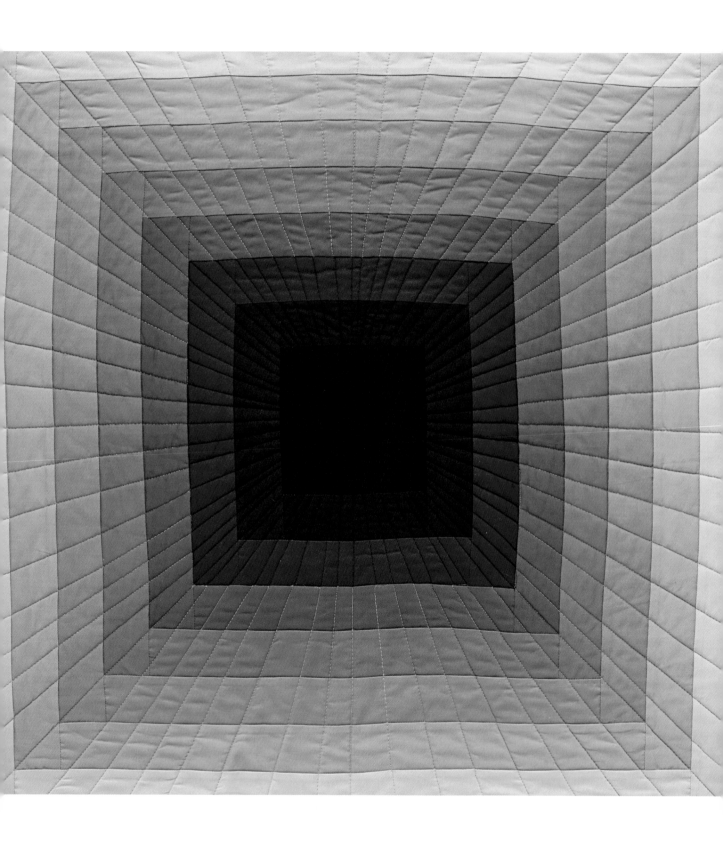

COLOR FRAMES

Designed and made by Amy Ellis and machine quilted by Natalia Bonner

Finished block size: 12″ × 12″, **Finished quilt size:** 70″ × 87″

The use of solid fabrics on a white background renders this quilt's geometric design wonderfully crisp and well defined. I really like the movement made by arranging the colors from light to dark in two color palettes, and then rotating the blocks. The light and dark areas allow the colors to create an alternate pattern within the quilt top.

Although it looks complex, once the cutting is finished, this quilt goes together quickly. Strip piecing the tiny squares speeds the process along.

To personalize the design, try using a different color palette; consider blues and greens, or yellows and blues, for example.

I set this quilt on point, with pieced half- and quarter-blocks instead of setting triangles. Also, instead of adding a border to frame the quilt, I used a wide, dark binding in Pepper, which I think is just the right touch. Instructions are included to achieve this look for your quilt as well.

MATERIALS AND SUPPLIES

White: 6⅜ yards

Pepper: ¾ yard

Ash: ¾ yard

Burgundy: ⅛ yard

Wine: ⅛ yard

Medium Pink: ⅛ yard

Pearl Pink: ⅛ yard

Windsor: ⅛ yard

Delft: ⅛ yard

Blueberry: ⅛ yard

Sky: ⅛ yard

Pomegranate: ¼ yard

Periwinkle: ¼ yard

Backing: 5½ yards

Batting: 78″ × 95″

Binding: 1¼ yards for extra-wide binding

CUTTING

White:

Cut 8 strips 8½″ × width of fabric (WOF); subcut into 32 squares 8½″ × 8½″ for the centers of the whole-blocks.

Cut 2 strips 8⅞″ × WOF; subcut into 7 squares 8⅞″ × 8⅞″ for the half-blocks. Cut each square on the diagonal once.

Cut 1 square 9¼″ × 9¼″. Cut the square on the diagonal twice for the quarter-blocks.

Cut 56 strips 1½″ × WOF; set aside 12 strips 1½″ × WOF for the long strip sets. Subcut the remainder into 64 strips 1½″ × 12½″ and 64 strips 1½″ × 10½″ for the framing strips within the whole blocks.

Cut 12 strips 1½″ × WOF; subcut into 24 strips 1½″ × 18″ for the short strip sets.

Cut 12 strips 1½″ × WOF; subcut into 28 strips 1½″ × 13″ for the framing strips within the half-blocks and 4 strips 1½″ × 14½″ for the framing strips within the quarter-blocks.

Pepper:

Cut 2 strips 3½″ × WOF for the strip sets. Set aside a strip for the long strip set, and from the other, subcut 1 rectangle 3½″ × 18″.

Cut 2 strips 4½″ × WOF. Save 1 strip for the long strip sets; from the other, subcut 1 rectangle 4½″ × 18″.

Cut 1 strip 5½″ × WOF; subcut into 2 rectangles 5½″ × 18″ for the half- and quarter-blocks.

Ash:

Cut 2 strips 3½″ × WOF. Save 1 strip for the long strip sets; from the other, subcut 1 rectangle 3½″ × 18″.

Cut 2 strips 4½″ × WOF. Save 1 strip for the long strip sets; from the other, subcut 1 rectangle 4½″ × 18″.

Cut 1 strip 5½″ × WOF; subcut into 2 rectangles 5½″ × 18″ for the half- and quarter-blocks.

Burgundy, Wine, Medium Pink, **Pearl Pink, Windsor, Delft,** Blueberry, **and Sky:**

Cut 2 strips 1½″ × WOF from each fabric. Save 1 strip of each fabric for the long strip sets; from the other, subcut 2 strips 1½″ × 18″.

Pomegranate and Periwinkle:

Cut 2 strips 1½″ × WOF from each fabric. Save 1 strip of each fabric for the long strip sets; from the other, subcut 2 strips 1½″ × 18″.

Cut an additional strip 1½″ × WOF from each fabric; subcut into 1 rectangle 1½″ × 18″ and 6 rectangles 1½″ × 2″ for the half- and quarter-block crosscut pieces. (You will have 2 extra periwinkle 1½″ × 2″ rectangles.)

Binding:

Cut 9 strips 4½″ × WOF. *

*This makes an extra-wide binding. If you want a standard-width binding, cut 9 strips 21/4″ × WOF.

INSTRUCTIONS

All seam allowances are ¼″.

This quilt has 32 whole-blocks, 14 half-blocks along the sides, and 4 quarter-blocks in the corners. Each block has a white center surrounded by multicolored small squares and rectangles, which are cut from strip sets.

NOTE

When strip piecing I like to use a shorter stitch length (usually 1.5mm) so that the stitches are less likely to pull apart when I'm handling the cut pieced units before sewing them in place.

Block assembly

For the blocks, make 1 each of strip sets A, B, C, and D at 40″ long, and 1 each at 18″ long. Make 1 each of strip sets E, F, G, and H at 18″ long. Press seams open. Crosscut the strip sets as follows:

Crosscut A, B, and C each into 36 units 1½″ wide.

Crosscut D into 34 units 1½″ wide.

Crosscut E, F, and H each into 4 units 1½″ wide.

Crosscut G into 6 units 1½″ wide.

When cutting the units, use the seams as a guide, ensuring that the cuts are perpendicular to the seams.

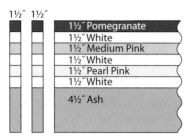

Set A—Cut 36.

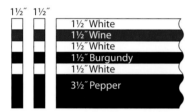

Set B—Cut 36.

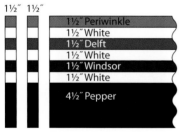

Set C—Cut 36.

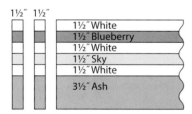

Set D—Cut 34.

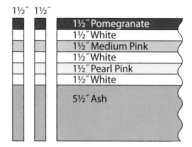

Set E—Cut 4.

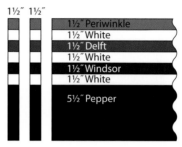

Set F—Cut 4.

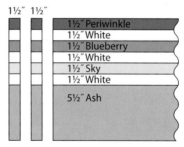

Set G—Cut 6.

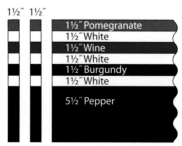

Set H—Cut 4.

Whole-blocks

1. Sew a D unit to the left side and a B unit to the right side of a White 8½″ × 8½″ square, oriented as shown, and press the seams open.

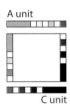

2. Add an A unit to the top of the block from Step 1 and a C unit to the bottom of the block, oriented as shown, and press the seams open.

3. Sew a White strip 1½″ × 10½″ to the left and right sides of the block, and a White strip 1½″ × 12½″ to the top and bottom, pressing the seams open as you go.

Make 32.

4. Repeat Steps 1–3 to make 32 blocks.

Half- and quarter-blocks

Some of the remaining crosscut units will be modified before they are added to the half- and quarter-triangles to complete the setting blocks.

1. Take the Periwinkle square off the end of a G unit; then sew the modified G unit to the short side of an 8⅞″ White half-square triangle, as shown in the U block diagram. Press the seam open.

2. Sew an F unit to the other short end of the unit from Step 1. Press the seam open.

3. Sew a White strip 1½″ × 13″ to both short sides of the unit from Step 2. Press the seams open. Trim the ends even with the long edge of the White triangle.

4. Repeat Steps 1–3 to make 4 half-blocks (U blocks).

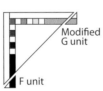

U block

Make 4.

5. Remove the Pomegranate square from the end of each of 4 H units. Repeat Steps 1–3 to make 4 half-blocks (V blocks) using the modified H units and 4 E units.

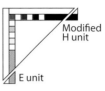

V block

Make 4.

6. Add a 1½″ × 2″ Periwinkle rectangle to the White square at the end of each of 2 D units. Repeat Steps 1–3 to make 2 half-blocks (W blocks) using the modified D units and 2 A units.

W block

Make 2.

7. Add a 1½″ × 2″ Pomegranate rectangle to the White square at the end of each of 4 B units. Repeat Steps 1–3 to make 4 half-blocks (X blocks) using the modified B units and 4 C units.

X block

Make 4.

Quilt top assembly

8. Remove the Periwinkle square from the end of a G unit and replace it with a 1½″ × 2″ Periwinkle rectangle. Sew the modified G unit to the long side of a 9¼″ quarter-square triangle. Press the seam open.

9. Add a 1½″ × 14½″ White strip next to the crosscut piece of the unit from Step 8.

10. Repeat Steps 8 and 9 to make 2 blocks (Y blocks).

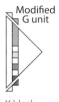

Y block

Make 2.

11. Remove the Pomegranate square from the end of an A unit, and replace it with a 1½″ × 2″ Pomegranate rectangle. Sew the modified A unit to the long side of a 9¼″ quarter-square triangle. Press the seam open.

12. Add a 1½″ × 14½″ White strip next to the crosscut piece of the unit from Step 11. Press.

13. Repeat Steps 11 and 12 to make 2 blocks (Z blocks).

Z block

Make 2.

Quilt assembly diagram

1. Lay out the blocks, orienting them as shown in the quilt assembly diagram.

2. Working on the diagonal, pin and sew the blocks into rows. Be sure each block is oriented properly. Press the seam allowances in opposite directions from row to row.

3. Pin and sew the rows together to complete the quilt top. Press the seam allowances all in the same direction.

Attaching a Wide Binding

1. Sew the 9 Pepper 4½˝ strips end to end, on the bias; press the seams open. Fold the binding in half lenthwise with wrong sides together, and then press. Do not trim the quilt top, backing, or batting yet.

2. Begin sewing on the binding along 1 side of the quilt top. Stop sewing ¼˝ away from the corner, and cut the binding, leaving a 2˝–3˝ tail to sew a miter. Fold the tail at a 45° angle. Continue adding binding, leaving a 2˝–3˝ tail at the start, beginning and stopping ¼˝ from each corner. Using a rotary cutter and a long ruler, trim the batting and backing 1˝ outside the seamline.

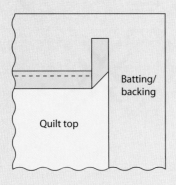

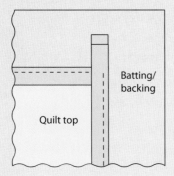

3. At each corner, measure the binding from the fold (A) to the binding seam (B). This should be about 2˝. Divide the measurement in half, and mark the halfway point (C) on the binding. Draw a 1˝ line from the halfway point toward the binding tail (D). Draw a line from A to D and from D to B. This is the stitching line. Repeat for each of the corners.

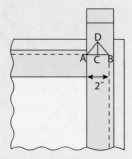

4. Carefully fold back the quilt on the diagonal, and pin the binding tails together. Using a tiny stitch length and backstitching at the beginning and end to secure the miter, sew along the marked line from A to D; pivot, and sew from D to B. Trim away excess, and fold over the corner. Secure the binding to the back of the quilt by hand with a blind stitch.

Quilting and finishing

1. Cut the backing fabric in half crosswise to create 2 pieces 95″ long. Remove the selvages, and sew the pieces together along their selvage edges. Press the seam allowance open.

2. Mark quilting designs on the quilt top, or plan to stitch without marking. I passed my quilt on to my favorite longarm quilter.

3. Use your preferred method or refer to Quiltmaking Basics (page 135) to layer and baste the quilt top, batting, and backing.

4. Quilt as desired. In my quilt, the concentric squares quilted within the White block centers add to the overall geometric nature of this quilt.

5. If you prefer the usual 2¼″ binding, use your preferred method or refer to Quiltmaking Basics. If you want to use my method to attach a wider binding, see the instructions on page 22.

KeYS

Designed and made by Alissa Haight Carlton

Keys is a graphic quilt based on a simple repeat of strips that reminds me of piano keys. This long, throw-sized quilt is perfect for any modern living room. I have chosen to use a group of neutral colors—Coal, Medium Grey, and Ivory—and one golden yellow—Butterscotch—to make a quilt that appeals to both masculine and feminine aesthetics.

I decided to quilt the piece in a way that would draw attention to the design created by the piecing. So I quilted a dense pattern of straight lines, filling in the pieced strips and leaving the open, negative "background" spaces unquilted.

To construct the quilt top, use strip piecing on a large scale. The fabric pieces might be larger than you are used to using, but they lend themselves to the bold, modern repeating design.

MATERIALS AND SUPPLIES

Coal: 2 yards (Fabric A)

Medium Grey: 1 yard (Fabric B)

Butterscotch: 1 yard (Fabric C)

Ivory: 1¼ yards (Fabric D)

Binding: ⅝ yard

Backing: 3⅝ yards*

Batting: 63″ × 84″

*If your fabric is less than 43″ wide, you will need additional fabric.

NOTE

Some pieces need to be longer than 40″. Piece together width-of-fabric (WOF) strips to build these longer pieces.

CUTTING

Coal (Fabric A):
Cut 5 pieces 32½″ × 10½″ (A1).

Cut 3 pieces 5″ × 10½″ (A2).

Cut 2 pieces 7½″ × 10½″ (A3).

Medium Grey (Fabric B):
Cut 1 piece 38½″ × 10½″ (B1).

Cut 1 piece 6½″ × 10½″ (B2).

Cut 1 piece 34½″ × 7½″ (B3).

Cut 1 piece 5½″ × 7½″ (B4).

Cut 1 piece 2½″ × 7½″ (B5).

Butterscotch (Fabric C):
Cut 1 piece 3½″ × 10½″ (C1).

Cut 2 pieces 3½″ × 7½″ (C2).

Cut 2 pieces 3½″ × 18½″ (C3).

Cut 3 pieces 62½″ × 3½″ (C4).

Cut 1 piece 3½″ × 19½″ (C5).

Ivory (Fabric D):
Cut 3 pieces 5″ × 4½″ (D1).

Cut 2 pieces 5″ × 5½″ (D2).

Cut 1 piece 5″ × 3½″ (D3).

Cut 10 pieces 34½″ × 1½″ (D4).

Cut 5 pieces 2½″ × 10½″ (D5).

Cut 2 pieces 62½″ × 1½″ (D6).

Cut 1 piece 62½″ × 2½″ (D7).

Binding:
Cut 8 strips 2½″ × WOF for double-fold binding.

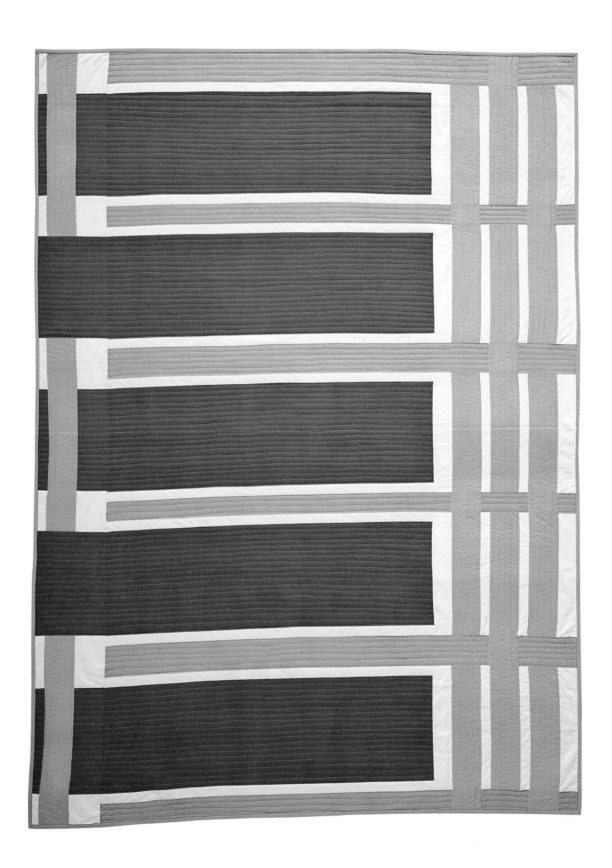

INSTRUCTIONS

All seam allowances are ¼″.

Quilt top assembly

Refer to the quilt assembly diagram (page 31). As you assemble the quilt top, sew with accurate ¼″ seam allowances so the final design lines up and "reads" correctly. Also note how you sew pieces together, and then cut those assembled units into smaller units.

1. Sew a D5 piece to the right side of each A1 piece.

2. Sew a D4 piece to the top and bottom (long) edges of each A1/D5 unit made in Step 1. Make 5. Set aside.

A1 unit

3. Sew together pieces B1, C1, and B2.

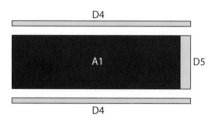

4. Cut the unit from Step 3 lengthwise into 3 strips 3½″ wide. Label these units E1 and set aside.

E1 units

5. Sew together B3, C2, B4, C2, and B5.

6. Then cut this unit from Step 5 lengthwise into 3 strips 2½″ wide. Label these units E2 and set aside.

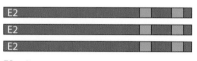

E2 units

7. Sew together C4, D6, C4, D6, C4, and D7. Then cut this unit crosswise into 5 pieces 12½″ wide. Label these units F and set aside.

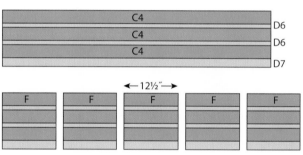

F units

8. Sew together D1, A2, and D1 as shown. Repeat for D2, A2, and D1 and for D2, A2, and D3. Cut each of these units into 2 strips, one 1½″ wide and the other 3½″ wide.

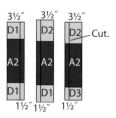

9. Sew piece C3 between the D1/A2/D1 pieces as shown. Repeat with C5 and D2/A2/D1 and with C3 and D2/A2/D3. Label the 3 new units G1, G2, and G3. Note that these are different from each other, so keep track of which is which.

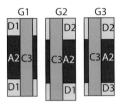

10. Refer to the quilt assembly diagram to sew the A1 units to the F units.

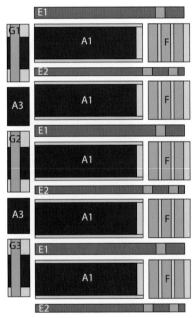

Quilt assembly diagram

11. Working top to bottom and being very careful to match seams so that the design elements are lined up, sew the E1 and E2 strips between the A1/F units as shown.

12. Again working from top to bottom, assemble G1, A3, G2, A3, and G3.

13. Taking care to make the pattern line up (pinning a lot helps!), sew the unit you made in Step 12 to the left side of the unit created in Step 11.

Quilting and finishing

1. Cut and piece the backing to make a piece 63″ × 84″.

2. Mark your quilting design on the quilt top, or plan to quilt without marking.

3. Use your favorite method or refer to Quiltmaking Basics (page 135) to layer and baste the quilt top, batting, and backing.

4. Quilt as desired. I machine quilted rows of straight lines, close together, across the Medium Grey and Butterscotch areas, leaving the Ivory background unquilted.

5. Sew together 288″ of double-fold binding. Use your favorite method or refer to Quiltmaking Basics to bind the quilt.

LADDERS

Designed and made by Elizabeth Hartman

Finished block size: 9″ × 9″, **Finished quilt size:** 63½″ × 81½″

I love to work with bright colors, and the color scheme is almost always the first thing I think about when planning a quilt. In this case, I started with rich, ever-so-slightly purple Kona Mahogany. I combined it with crisp Snow and a palette of beautiful sunset colors in Amber, Cayenne, Brick, Orange, Pomegranate, Papaya, and School Bus. I chose to use Mahogany fabric for the binding. This creates a tiny border around the front of the quilt, without adding a wider conventional border. On the quilt back, the Mahogany contrasts nicely with the bright colors and creates a beautiful frame.

The pieced ladders in each block are perhaps an unusual patchwork motif, but I really enjoy them. The shape is simple and graphic, but the recognizable object suggests movement all around the quilt top. The rungs on the lad-ders are slightly different sizes, and the ladders themselves are a little off-center in each block. I planned them this way to avoid a look that was too perfect and orderly—to achieve a "wonky without being wonky" look.

I like to create quilt backs that are a secondary composition, complementary to the look of the quilt top. In this case, I took the ladder shapes and bright colors from the quilt blocks and expanded them to fit the quilt back. The result is two extra-large pieced ladders and a lot of big, bright blocks of color.

I think this design would look equally fabulous in other color schemes. Navy and White with a sea of Cobalt, Teal, and Aqua could be cool and crisp. Charcoal and Ash with a range of violets could be sharp and sophisticated. Pick your favorite colors and run with them!

MATERIALS AND SUPPLIES

Mahogany: 2½ yards for blocks and quilt back

Snow: 3¼ yards for blocks and quilt back

Cayenne: 2½ yards for blocks and quilt back

Amber and School Bus: 1½ yards each for blocks and quilt back

Brick and Orange: 1 yard each for blocks and quilt back

Pomegranate and Papaya: ⅞ yard each for blocks and quilt back

Binding: ⅝ yard

Batting: 72″ × 90″ (I used Warm & Natural.)

Labels or blue tape for labeling cut pieces

4 plastic bags for organizing cut pieces

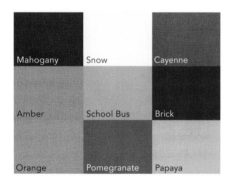

CUTTING

> # NOTE
>
> As you cut, it's important to keep all the pieces for the quilt top blocks and the quilt back organized. For the blocks, sort the strips into 4 groups by size, as indicated in the cutting instructions. Place them in 4 plastic bags labeled Bag 1 through Bag 4. For the 40 backing pieces, use labels or tape and a marker to label each cut piece with a different letter code, as indicated in the cutting instructions.

Mahogany:
For the blocks:

Cut 35 strips 2″ × WOF (width of fabric).

For the quilt back:

Cut 1 strip 14½″ × WOF. Subcut into 1 piece 14½″ × 11½″ (label it Q2), 1 piece 14½″ × 7″ (label it M2), and 1 piece 10½″ × 9½″ (label it F2).

Snow:
Cut 35 strips 1¼″ × WOF for the blocks.

Cut 1 strip 6½″ × WOF. Subcut 2 pieces 6½″ × 10½″ for the quilt back. (Label 1 piece E and the other E2.)

Cut 5 strips 4½″ × length of remaining fabric (about 52″). Trim 4 strips to 4½″ × 50½″ for the quilt back. (Label the pieces I, I2, J, and J2.) Subcut the remaining strip into 4 pieces 4½″ × 10½″ for the quilt back. (Label the pieces B, B2, G, and G2.) Fold the remaining fabric in half, and cut along the fold to create 2 large rectangles; square them up to 18″ × 25″. Subcut the rectangles into 7 strips 1¼″ × 25″, 7 strips 1½″ × 25″, and 7 strips 1¾″ × 25″ for the quilt blocks.

Cayenne:
For the quilt back:

Cut 1 strip 24½″ × WOF. Trim to 24½″ × 36″ (label T).

Cut 1 strip 15½″ × WOF. Trim to 15½″ × 36″ (label S).

Cut 1 strip 18½″ × WOF. Subcut into 1 piece 18½″ × 11½″ (label O), 1 piece 18½″ × 7″ (label K), 1 piece 10½″ × 9½″ (label A), and 1 piece 10½″ × 5½″ (label C).

Cut 1 strip 11½″ × WOF. Subcut into 1 piece 11½″ × 11½″ (label R), 1 piece 10½″ × 8½″ (label H), and 1 piece 11½″ × 7″ (label N).

For the blocks:

Cut 1 strip 2″ × WOF. Cut 1 strip 1¾″ × WOF and trim to 1¾″ × 25″. Pin the 2 strips together and place in Bag 1.

Cut 1 strip 3″ × WOF. Cut 1 strip 2″ × WOF and trim to 2″ × 25″. Pin the 2 strips together and place in Bag 2.

Cut 1 strip 2½″ × WOF. Cut 1 strip 1¾″ × WOF and trim to 1¾″ × 25″. Pin the 2 strips together and place in Bag 3.

Cut 1 strip 3½″ × WOF. Cut 1 strip 2½″ × WOF and trim to 2½″ × 25″. Pin the 2 strips together and place in Bag 4.

School Bus: *
For the quilt back:

Cut 1 strip 15½″ × WOF. Trim to 15½″ × 36″ (label S2).

Cut 1 strip 18½″ × WOF. Subcut into 1 piece 18½″ × 11½″ (label O2), 1 piece 18½″ × 7″ (label K2), 1 piece 10½″ × 9½″ (label A2), and 1 piece 10½″ × 5½″ (label C2).

Amber: *
For the quilt back:

Cut 1 strip 24½″ × WOF. Trim to 24½″ × 36″ (label T2).

Cut 1 strip 11½″ × WOF. Subcut into 1 piece 11½″ × 11½″ (label R2), 1 piece 11½″ × 7″ (label N2), and 1 piece 10½″ × 8½″ (label H2).

Brick: *
For the quilt back:

Cut 1 strip 14½″ × WOF. Subcut into 1 piece 14½″ × 11½″ (label Q2), 1 piece 14½″ × 7″ (label M2), and 1 piece 10½″ × 9½″ (label F2).

Orange: *
For the quilt back:

Cut 1 strip 14½″ × WOF. Subcut into 1 piece 14½″ × 11½″ (label Q), 1 piece 14½″ × 7″ (label M), and 1 piece 10½″ × 9½″ (label F).

Pomegranate: *
For the quilt back:

Cut 1 strip 7½″ × WOF. Subcut into 1 piece 7½″ × 11½″ (label P2), 1 piece 7½″ × 7″ (label L2), and 1 piece 5½″ × 10½″ (label D2).

Papaya: *
For the quilt back:

Cut 1 strip 7½″ × WOF. Subcut into 1 piece 7½″ × 11½″ (label P), 1 piece 7½″ × 7″ (label L), and 1 piece 5½″ × 10½″ (label D).

After cutting the quilt back pieces, follow the steps for the Cayenne fabric to cut strips for the blocks, and place them in the 4 plastic bags. When you are finished, each bag should contain 7 same-sized strip pairs—1 pair each of the 7 colors.

Binding:
Cut 8 strips 2½″ × WOF.

INSTRUCTIONS

All seam allowances are ¼″, and all seams are pressed open.

Making the blocks

1. Select 1 pair of pinned strips from each of the 4 bags. Unpin each pair and set the shorter (25″) strips aside. Create a 9½″-wide strip set by sewing the longer strips together in the following order: 2″ strip from Bag 1, 3″ strip from Bag 2, 2½″ strip from Bag 3, and 3½″ strip from Bag 4.

2. Subcut the strip set into 9 pieced units 1½″ × 9½″ and 9 pieced units 2″ × 9½″. These units will go on either side of each ladder.

1½″ 2″

Cut 9 units 2″ wide and 9 units 1½″ wide.

3. Create a second 9½″-wide strip set using the 25″ strips you set aside in Step 1, plus 3 strips of Snow fabric—1 each of 1¼″ × 25″, 1½″ × 25″, and 1¾″ × 25″. Sew the strips together in the following order: 1¾″ strip from Bag 1, 1¼″ strip of Snow fabric, 2″ strip from Bag 2, 1½″ strip of Snow fabric, 1¾″ strip from Bag 3, 1¾″ strip of Snow fabric, and 2½″ strip from Bag 4.

4. Subcut the strip set into 9 pieced units 9½″ × 2½″. These units will be the rungs at the center of each ladder.

2½″

Cut 9 units 2½″ wide.

5. Chain piece a 9½″ side of each rung unit from Step 4 to a 1¼″ × WOF strip of Snow fabric as shown. (Keep any excess Snow fabric for future chain piecing.) Cut the Snow fabric between each 2 rung units.

Cut.

6. Repeat Step 5 to sew a 1¼″ × WOF strip of Snow fabric to the other 9½″ side of each unit, creating a ladder shape. Trim each unit to 9½″ × 4″.

7. Sew a 2″ × 9½″ unit from Step 2 to the left side of a ladder unit. Sew a 1½″ × 9½″ unit from Step 2 to the right side of the same ladder unit. Repeat with the remaining units to make a total of 9. Be sure the colors are aligned across the ladder.

8. Chain piece the 9½″ side of each block to a Mahogany strip 2″ × WOF. Trim each block to 9½″ × 9½″.

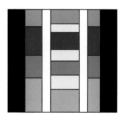

9. Repeat Steps 1–8 to create 6 more sets of 9 blocks each, for a total of 63 blocks.

Making the quilt top

Using the quilt photo (page 35) as a reference, arrange the blocks in 9 rows of 7 blocks each, rotating every other block 90°. Sew the blocks in each row together; then sew the rows together to complete the quilt top.

Making the quilt back

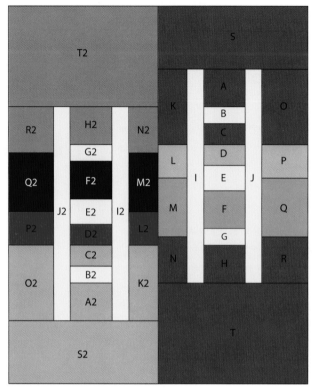

Quilt back assembly diagram

1. Sew pieces A, B, C, D, E, F, G, and H together, in alphabetical order, matching 10½˝ sides.

2. Sew pieces I and J to the sides of the pieced unit from Step 1 to create a ladder shape. Set aside.

3. Sew pieces K, L, M, and N together, in alphabetical order, matching 7˝ sides.

4. Sew pieces O, P, Q, and R together, in alphabetical order, matching 11½˝ sides.

5. Sew the K/L/M/N unit to the left side of the ladder unit from Step 2.

6. Sew the O/P/Q/R unit to the right-hand side of the unit from Step 5.

7. Sew piece S to the top and piece T to the bottom of the unit from Step 6 to finish half of the quilt back.

8. Repeat Steps 1–7 with pieces A2 through T2 to make the other half of the quilt back (A2 corresponds to A, B2 corresponds to B, etc.).

9. Complete the quilt back by sewing the 2 halves together, matching the sides bordered by the 7″-wide pieced units. (The ladders will be offset from each other, and the color-blocked areas of each half will not line up.)

Quilting and finishing

1. Mark a quilting design on the quilt top, or plan to stitch without marking.

2. Use your favorite method or refer to Quilt-making Basics (page 135) to layer and baste the quilt top, batting, and backing.

3. Quilt as desired. I free-motion quilted my quilt on my home machine using a blocky, meandering pattern. In a quilt like this one, where there is a lot of contrast between light and dark, I choose thread that most closely matches the lightest part of the composition. In this case, I chose a peachy color that doesn't show up too much on the Snow but is less stark on the Mahogany than an off-white thread would have been.

4. Use your favorite method or refer to Quilt-making Basics to join the binding strips with diagonal seams and bind the quilt.

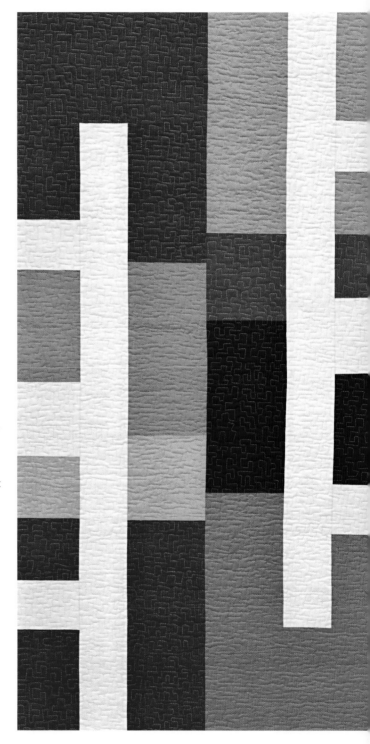

LADY OF THE LAKE

Designed and made by Rita Hodge

Finished block size: 7½″ × 7½″, **Finished quilt size:** 53″ × 68″

History has it that the Lady of the Lake quilt block got its name from the title of a popular narrative poem published in 1810 by Scottish author Sir Walter Scott. American pioneer men and women loved Scott's heroic tales, and quilters honored him by naming a patchwork block after his Lady of the Lake. This traditional design is still widely used by many modern-day quilters. It is equally well suited for traditional and reproduction fabrics and for bright, colorful modern fabrics.

The block is easy to piece and requires as a minimum just two fabrics arranged as a positive and a negative (light and dark). All components are half-square triangles—simple blocks of two large half-square triangles alternating with more complex blocks.

This design is a great way to use scraps and can be made in a myriad of colorways. I have chosen a cheerful and modern green/blue palette for the larger half-square triangles and have surrounded these blocks with an array of colorful triangles that sparkle against the fresh white background fabric.

MATERIALS AND SUPPLIES

White: 2¾ yards for the blocks

Chartreuse: 1½ yards for the blocks

Azure: 1 fat quarter or ⅜ yard for the blocks

Peacock: 1 fat quarter or ⅜ yard for the blocks

Assorted colors: about 1½ yards for the blocks*

Backing: 3⅝ yards

Binding: ½ yard

Batting: 61″ × 76″

Or use a Kaufman Roll-Up in Kona Cotton Solids (Classic Palette, Bright Palette, or some of each). They contain approximately 40 strips 2½″ wide.

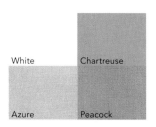

CUTTING

White:
Cut 16 squares 8⅜″ × 8⅜″ for Block A.

Cut 16 squares 5⅜″ × 5⅜″ for Block B.

Cut 16 strips 2½″ × 40″; crosscut each strip into 16 squares 2½″ × 2½″, for a total of 256 squares for Block B.

Chartreuse:
Cut 14 squares 8⅜″ × 8⅜″ for Block A.

Cut 15 squares 5⅜″ × 5⅜″ Block B.

Azure:
Cut 1 square 8⅜″ × 8⅜″ for Block A.

Cut 1 square 5⅜″ × 5⅜″ for Block B.

Peacock:
Cut 1 square 8⅜″ × 8⅜″ for Block A.

Cut 1 square 5⅜″ × 5⅜″ for Block B.

Assorted colors:
Cut 16 strips 2½″ × width of fabric. Subcut each strip into 16 squares 2½″ × 2½″ for a total of 256 squares. If using a Kona Cotton Solids Roll-Up, crosscut strips into 256 squares 2½″ × 2½″.

Binding:
Cut 7 strips 2¼″ × 40″ for double-fold binding.

INSTRUCTIONS

All seam allowances are ¼˝.

Block assembly

To piece the half-square triangles, refer to Piecing Half-Square Triangles (below).

This quilt is made from 2 alternating blocks—Block A and Block B.

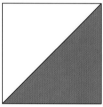

Block A

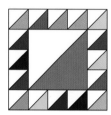

Block B

Block A

Piece the half-square triangle blocks using all the 8⅜˝ × 8⅜˝ Chartreuse, Azure, and Peacock squares, each paired with a White square of the same size, to make 31 Block A units. You will have an extra Peacock and White half-square triangle.

Block B

1. For the block center, pair the 5⅜˝ × 5⅜˝ Chartreuse, Azure, and Peacock squares with White squares of the same size to make half-square triangles, as for Block A. Each unit will measure 5˝ × 5˝ before being sewn into the block. Make 32 units, and set aside. You will have extra Chartreuse and Peacock units.

2. For the block borders, pair the 256 white squares 2½˝ × 2½˝ with 256 assorted color squares 2½˝ × 2½˝ to make 512 half-square triangles. Carefully press and trim each finished unit to 2˝ × 2˝.

NOTE

Accurate piecing is important when sewing small squares. Take time to sew accurate ¼˝ seams, and press carefully. The cutting sizes for this part of the process are oversized, and each completed half-square triangle requires trimming to an accurate 2˝ × 2˝.

Piecing Half-Square Triangles

1. Place a piece 1 square on a piece 2 square with right sides together. With a water-soluble fabric marker, draw a diagonal line on the wrong side of the top square, from corner to corner.

Piece 1
Piece 2

2. Sew a ¼˝ seam on either side of the drawn line.

3. Cut along the center line. Press to the dark side.

3. Sew 192 of the 2″ × 2″ units into 64 sets of 3 for the top and bottom block borders. Ensure correct orientation as shown. Press all seams in the same direction.

Top and bottom block border

4. Sew together 320 of the 2″ × 2″ units into 64 sets of 5 for the side block borders. Ensure correct orientation. Press all seams in the same direction.

Side block border

5. Sew top and bottom borders to the 5″ × 5″ center units; then sew on the side borders. Press all seams toward the center. Repeat to make a total of 32 blocks.

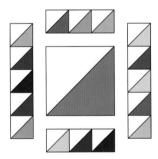

Quilt top assembly

1. Arrange all the blocks on a design wall or flat surface. Start with Block B in the top left corner of the quilt, and alternate blocks going across the rows, ensuring correct block orientation as shown in the quilt assembly diagram. Lay out 9 rows of 7 blocks each, alternating the beginning block in each row.

2. Sew blocks together into rows. Press the seams toward the A blocks.

3. Sew the rows together. Press the seams downward.

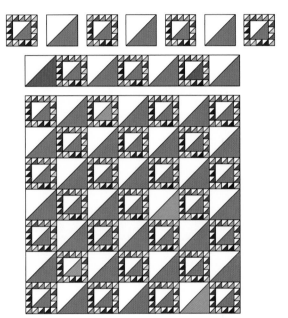

Quilt assembly diagram

Quilting and finishing

1. Mark quilting designs on the quilt top, or plan to stitch without marking.

2. Use your preferred method or refer to Quiltmaking Basics (page 135) to layer and baste the quilt top, batting, and backing.

3. Quilt as desired by hand or machine. I quilted a simple diagonal grid.

4. Refer to Quiltmaking Basics or use your preferred method to bind the quilt.

LITTLE LANDSCAPES

Designed and made by Jean Wells

Finished quilt sizes: 10½″ × 10½″ and 11¼″ × 9″

These two little landscape quilts are a perfect way to capture the simple lines of the land as well as the colors of a natural setting. Each of these pieces features a different part of the landscape in Oregon, where I live and work.

You can learn a lot about color by studying natural landscapes during different times of the day. You'll see slight changes, such as two shades of blue in the sky. You can capture these shades in a quilt using narrow bands of color that are lighter, darker, or brighter than the colors around them.

These pieces feature simple line work that doesn't detract from the beauty of the forms inspired by the land. Abstracting the shapes creates a dramatic statement of form and color. Each quilt presents a different color story and is worked intuitively. Your quilt will not end up exactly like mine. Strips, squares, and rectangles are cut without rulers. As you work, the shapes created by the lines that you cut will be unique to you.

Cascade
Mountains

Finished quilt size: 10½″ × 10½″

Ocean Sunset

Finished quilt size: 11¼″ × 9″

GENERAL INSTRUCTIONS

Follow these general cutting and piecing instructions for both quilts. Details for the individual quilts are listed with each project.

MATERIALS AND SUPPLIES

The specific fabrics used in each quilt are listed with the project roughly in order, beginning at the top of the piece and working down.

⅓ yard of your favorite color listed for the piecing and backing

⅛ yard of each remaining color listed

⅓ yard of thin batting

⅜″-diameter wooden dowel for hanging

NOTE

When choosing fabric, think about the layers of color in much the same way that a painter does. For example, two or three blues are better than one. To build up your stash of solids, buy ⅛ yard of as many solid fabrics as you can get your hands on, or check out Kaufman's Kona fat-quarter bundles available in ten different color families. This will ensure a wide range of color choices for you to have as you work.

Note that while most of the fabrics in these quilts are Kona Cotton Solids, some accent pieces of Kaufman's Carolina Chambray Shot Cotton are also included.

Cutting and piecing

To cut the pieces, use sharp scissors or a small or medium rotary cutter with a new blade.

To make either of these quilts, begin by laying out a mock-up using strips and squares in the colors you propose. Cut strips and squares approximately 1½″ to 2″ wide, referring to the quilt assembly diagram (page 53 or 55) to determine the strip widths. Some areas will need wider pieces, some narrower—use your own judgment to determine what looks best. Where you want detail, smaller squares or rectangles can be cut and pieced together into strips. You will trim all these pieces before you stitch them together.

1. Refer to each quilt assembly diagram to determine the approximate length and width of each strip. Add 1½″ to each measurement. Finished measurements are given at each side of the diagrams as a guideline. Yours will be approximately this size.

2. Experiment until you are satisfied with the arrangement and colors. Then follow the steps in Piecing Gentle Curves (page 50) to make the quilt. You can begin at the bottom or the top of the quilt.

3. Some of the strips are made up of several smaller squares and rectangles. Piece the sections in these strips together, and press. Then stitch them to the next strip. Refer to the assembly diagrams for each of the quilts.

4. Continue trimming and adding strips in the same manner until you have completed the quilt top. As you piece the strips, the ends will be uneven. The quilt will be trimmed when finished.

Piecing Gentle Curves

1. Lay the first strip right side up, and cut along an edge in a gentle line that is not too curvy or too straight. Pull away the excess fabric.

2. Place the first strip (right side up) on top of the second strip (right side up) so the raw edge of the first strip just barely covers the raw edge of the second strip. Use the line of the first strip as a pattern for cutting the line on the second strip. Pull away excess fabric of the second strip from under the first strip.

3. Place the second strip on top of the first strip with right sides together. This will seem awkward, and the edges will not match up, but don't worry. Go to the sewing machine and place the 2 fabrics under the presser foot. Using approximately a ¼˝ seam allowance, stitch about 1˝ along the edge, keeping the raw edges together.

4. For the remainder of the seam, hold the top fabric in your left hand and lay it down on the bottom fabric, lining up the raw edges as you stitch. (The right hand can move the bottom fabric at the same time so the raw edges line up on top of each other.) The top fabric will pull slightly as you stitch; this will press out. Press the seam in one direction.

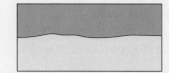

Quilting and finishing

1. Press the pieced landscape. Place it right side up on the batting, smooth it out, and pin in 6–8 places.

2. Quilt with a thread that is close to the color of the fabrics. You can use a walking foot or free-motion quilt using an embroidery foot to machine quilt through the layers, adding detail lines and motifs. Refer to the photo of each quilt (page 48) for ideas on how to quilt it.

3. Referring to the quilt dimensions, trim the quilt ½˝ larger than the finished size in both length and width. Cut a backing the same size. Place the quilt and backing right sides together, and stitch around the edges using a ¼˝ seam allowance. Leave a 3˝ opening on the bottom edge for turning. Trim the corners and turn to the right side. You may need to use a blunt tool to push out the corners.

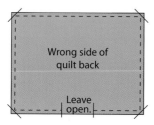

4. Place the right side of the quilt on your ironing board. Set your iron on steam, and press the edges around the quilt, making sure the backing rolls toward the back and does not show on the front. Hand stitch to close the opening.

5. Cut a dowel 1˝ shorter than the width of the finished quilt. Center the dowel ¾˝ from the top edge of the quilt. Use a double sewing thread, knotted at the end, to tack the dowel to the quilt in several places. Hang by resting the dowel on a couple of small nails.

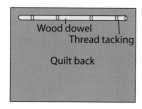

Cascade Mountains

This quilt has a set-in piece in the top strip that represents a snowy peak of the Cascades mountain range.

FABRICS

Listed from top to bottom of the quilt

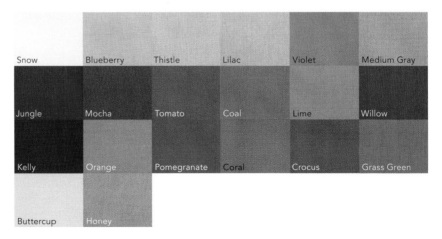

Snow	Blueberry	Thistle	Lilac	Violet	Medium Gray
Jungle	Mocha	Tomato	Coal	Lime	Willow
Kelly	Orange	Pomegranate	Coral	Crocus	Grass Green
Buttercup	Honey				

MAKING THE QUILT

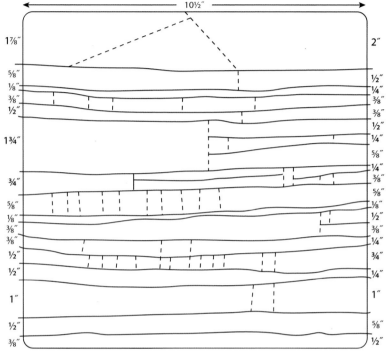

Quilt assembly diagram

1. Follow the general instructions (page 49) to cut and sew together the strips. Several strips are pieced from 2 or more different fabrics; piece them first before trimming and sewing them to the quilt top.

2. To make the mountain, cut the mountain shape from the Snow fabric. Lay the sky fabric under the mountain, and cut along the left side of the mountain through the sky fabric. Stitch the seam, and press toward the mountain. Trim off the sky fabric that extends above the mountain as shown. Repeat the process on the right side of the mountain.

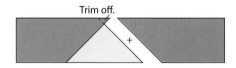

3. Follow Steps 1–5 under Quilting and Finishing (page 51) to complete the quilt.

Ocean Sunset

This quilt has several areas where smaller pieces are joined to make a strip. It also features a slim insert where the seam disappears.

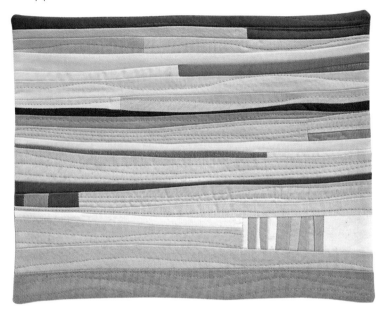

FABRICS

Listed from top to bottom and left to right in the quilt

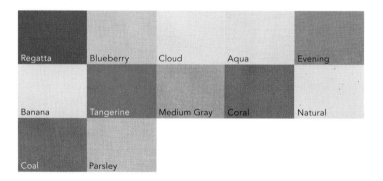

Regatta	Blueberry	Cloud	Aqua	Evening
Banana	Tangerine	Medium Gray	Coral	Natural
Coal	Parsley			

MAKING THE QUILT

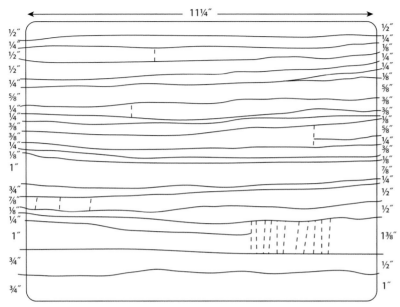

Quilt assembly diagram

1. Follow the General Instructions (page 49) to cut and sew together the strips. Several strips are pieced from 2 or 3 different fabrics; piece them first before trimming and sewing them to the quilt top.

2. To make the third strip from the bottom, see the illustration below. Sew strip 1 to strip 2; then sew on pieces 3–12. Press. Sew the 2 sections together, press, and sew the strip to the quilt.

3. Just down from the top right side of the quilt there is a slim dark red piece of fabric where the seam disappears. To achieve this look, first add a narrow piece of fabric to one end of a strip. Press the seam. Then join this to the next piece of fabric as shown, and a slim insert will appear.

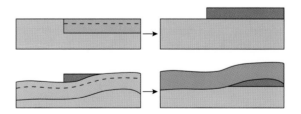

4. Follow Steps 1–5 under Quilting and Finishing (page 51) to complete the quilt.

LUPINe

Designed and made by Emily Cier and quilted by Cathy Kirk

Finished quilt sizes: Lap 60″ × 60″, twin 76″ × 96″, queen 96″ × 96″

This quilt design is half modern, half whimsical, and all octagons. It looks like a sea of bubbles, and lines of elevation on a topological map, and a pond of purple lily pads, all at once. Best of all, it's not hard to make, despite how intricate it looks. It's broken down into very simple rectangular strips, squares, and half-square triangles. As long as you're detail oriented, it doesn't require anything more than novice quilting skills— or anything above a C+ in geometry class.

You'll find instructions here for three different sizes, from lap to queen, so pick whichever will work best for your room.

Picking Kona Cotton palettes is as personal a choice as the right wine or the perfect flower. This set of purples in varied shades gives the quilt a rich, playful springtime vibe. But really, this quilt is a canvas that could have a hundred different moods, so try your hand at picking your own bold palette!

MATERIALS

Yardage is based on fabric that is at least 40″ wide.

FABRIC	Lap	Twin	Queen
A: Cerise	⅞ yard	1½ yards	1⅝ yards
B: Parsley	⅔ yard	1 yard	1⅛ yards
C: Petunia	1¼ yards	2⅓ yards	2⅞ yards
D: Snow	1¼ yards	2 yards	2½ yards
E: Caribbean	¾ yard	1⅛ yards	1½ yards
F: Lupine	1⅛ yards	1½ yards	1¾ yards
G: Eggplant	1⅛ yards	1⅝ yards	1¾ yards
Batting	68″ × 68″	84″ × 104″	104″ × 104″
Backing: Petunia	4⅓ yards	6⅛ yards*	9⅛ yards
Binding: Cerise	⅝ yard	⅞ yard	1 yard

Requires 42″-wide fabric

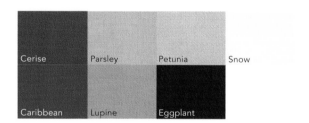

Cerise   Parsley   Petunia   Snow

Caribbean   Lupine   Eggplant

Lap size pictured, 60″ × 60″.

CUTTING

Cutting instructions in the charts are for rectangles and half-square triangles (HSTs). Instructions include 1 extra strip in case of mistakes. I recommend cutting all of the pieces for the quilt before you start sewing.

RECTANGLES

Quilt size: Lap

FABRIC	A	B	C	D	E	F	G
FIRST CUT: Cut 2½″ × width of fabric (WOF) strips from each fabric.							
2½″ × WOF	6	4	10	9	5	8	9
SECOND CUT							
30½″							1
26½″							2
24½″							1
22½″							1
18½″							1
16½″			1				1
14½″			3				
12½″						2	1
10½″	2	1	1	6	1	7	
8½″			4	1	4		7
6½″	5	3	12	5	3	7	3
4½″		3	16	24	1	1	4
2½″	49	19	34	28	22	36	14

NOTE

For the second cuts, start with the longest subcut, and then cut each longest remaining subcut possible from the leftover portion, cutting smaller and smaller pieces until the strip is too small to be useful. Continue with the remaining strips until all subcuts for that fabric have been made. As you cut, line up the piles of pieces in alphabetical order and label them for easy reference.

Quilt size: Twin

FABRIC	A	B	C	D	E	F	G
FIRST CUT: Cut 2½″ × width of fabric (WOF) strips from each fabric.							
2½″ × WOF	11	7	22	16	8	11	14
SECOND CUT							
30½″							1
26½″							2
24½″							1
22½″							1
20½″	1						
18½″							1
16½″	1		2		1		1
14½″	1		3				
12½″	1		4		1	2	1
10½″	2	3	4	10	1	9	
8½″	2	1	23	3	7	2	15
6½″	9	12	27	14	4	9	8
4½″	2	5	32	47	14	3	8
2½″	77	32	49	62	34	72	33

Quilt size: Queen

FABRIC	A	B	C	D	E	F	G
FIRST CUT: Cut 2½″ × width of fabric (WOF) strips from each fabric.							
2½″ × WOF	13	8	28	21	11	14	16
SECOND CUT							
30½″			1				1
26½″			1				2
24½″							1
22½″			2			1	1
20½″	1						
18½″			2	2			1
16½″	1		3		1	1	1
14½″	1		4	2			2
12½″	1		2		4	2	1
10½″	2	3	2	10	2	9	2
8½″	3	2	22	5	8	4	15
6½″	15	14	30	17	6	9	13
4½″	3	8	51	61	17	5	8
2½″	89	37	56	67	46	89	34

SQUARES FOR MAKING HALF-SQUARE TRIANGLES

Quilt size: Lap

FABRIC

A	B	C	D	E	F	G
FIRST CUT (STRIPS): Cut 2⅞″ × WOF strips from each fabric.						
3	2	4	4	2	3	2
SECOND CUT (SQUARES): Cut 2⅞″ × 2⅞″ squares from above strips.						
35	16	45	45	22	32	23

Quilt size: Twin

FABRIC

A	B	C	D	E	F	G
FIRST CUT (STRIPS): Cut 2⅞″ × WOF strips from each fabric.						
6	3	7	8	4	5	4
SECOND CUT (SQUARES): Cut 2⅞″ × 2⅞″ squares from above strips.						
65	36	85	94	51	59	52

Quilt size: Queen

FABRIC

A	B	C	D	E	F	G
FIRST CUT (STRIPS): Cut 2⅞″ × WOF strips from each fabric.						
6	4	8	9	6	6	5
SECOND CUT (SQUARES): Cut 2⅞″ × 2⅞″ squares from above strips.						
76	43	102	116	66	74	61

NOTE

Cut the strips and subcut them into squares as described in the charts. The squares will be used to create the half-square triangles in the next step.

INSTRUCTIONS

All seam allowances are ¼″. Precise piecing is necessary to make sure the pieces stay aligned. To piece the half-square triangles, refer to Piecing Half-Square Triangles (page 44). You don't have to press as you go along—unless you really love to iron!

Half-square triangle assembly

Refer to the Half-Square Triangle Assembly chart to combine the 2⅞″ × 2⅞″ squares into HSTs. The combinations will yield twice as many HSTs as the starting number of squares of each color. For example, 6 C squares (piece 1) plus 6 B squares (piece 2) will yield 12 C/B HSTs. Some quilt sizes use an odd number of HST color combinations, so you may have a few left over when the quilt top is complete.

Strip assembly

The quilt assembly diagram (page 64) gives the width for the pieces used in each strip. (Strips are cut 2½″ high.) When no width is given, use a 2½″-wide piece.

Chain piecing is the simplest way to sew the strips. Note that some pieces are HSTs. Piece all the strips for a single quilt section before moving on to the next section.

1. Sew piece 1 to piece 2, piece 3 to piece 4, piece 5 to piece 6, and so forth, in a chain. Then go back and snip the thread in between each pair of units.

HALF-SQUARE TRIANGLE ASSEMBLY

Quilt size: Lap

PIECE 2	PIECE 1					
	A	B	C	D	E	F
B						
C	14	4				
D	14	6	5			
E	2	2	4	6		
F	3	1	5	12	8	
G	2	3	13	2		3

Quilt size: Twin

PIECE 2	PIECE 1					
	A	B	C	D	E	F
B	1					
C	24	7				
D	18	11	14			
E	9	8	11	13		
F	6	2	14	23	9	
G	8	7	15	16	1	5

Quilt size: Queen

PIECE 2	PIECE 1					
	A	B	C	D	E	F
B	2					
C	29	8				
D	19	12	20			
E	12	10	13	16		
F	7	2	17	29	13	
G	8	9	15	21	2	6

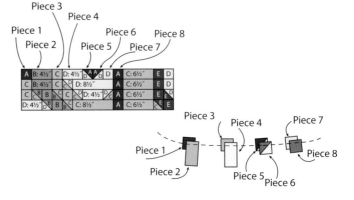

2. Continue chain piecing by sewing Unit 1/2 to Unit 3/4, Unit 5/6 to Unit 7/8, and so forth.

3. Snip and continue to sew units together until you've completed the entire strip.

4. Set the strip aside until you have completed all the strips for that section.

Quilt top assembly

1. When all the strips in the first section are complete, press the seams in the first strip in the same direction. Press seams in the opposite direction for the next strip. Sew the strips together to form the first section, backstitching to secure the seams at the beginning and end of each strip.

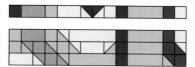

Portion of top left section

2. Sew the next set of strips, press adjacent rows in opposite directions, and then sew those together into the next section. Continue until all of the sections are complete.

3. Sew the completed sections together and press.

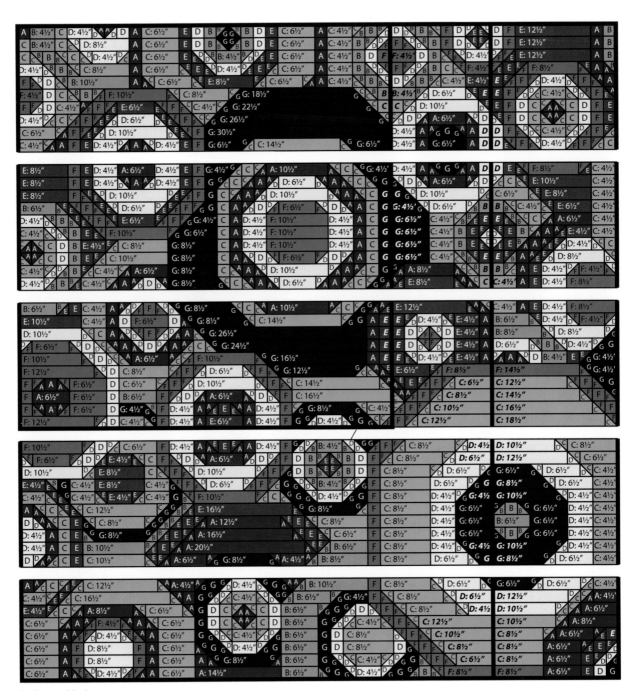

Quilt assembly diagram

NOTE

The quilt assembly diagram contains all three quilt sizes, with lines showing the edges of each size. When piecing a quilt larger than lap size, various pieces will be bisected along the smaller quilts' borders. Where two pieces of the same fabric meet across the border, you should combine those two diagram rectangles (noted in bold italic type) and use a piece corresponding to the combined size (taking into account seam allowances). For instance, if you are constructing a queen quilt, and the twin quilt border divides two F pieces (F: 4½˝ and F: 2½˝), you should instead use a single F piece (F: 6½˝). The cutting chart assumes you will make this substitution and includes the larger, combined pieces rather than the smaller, divided pieces.

Quilting and finishing

1. Mark quilting designs on the quilt top or plan to stitch without marking.

2. Cut and piece your backing fabric. Use your preferred method or refer to Quiltmaking Basics (page 135) to layer and baste the quilt top, batting, and backing.

3. Quilt as desired by hand or machine. My quilt features a repeating fan motif that adds lots of texture.

4. Refer to Quiltmaking Basics or use your preferred method to bind the quilt.

MODERN CROSS

Designed and made by Kathy Mack

Finished block size: 10½″ × 10½″, **Finished quilt size:** 45″ × 45″

This quilt is a study in nines. Each block is based on the traditional Nine-Patch block design. The quilt is made up of nine blocks using a color formula of nine different Kona Cotton colors. Each color appears in the quilt three times—once as the cross, once as the middle square background, and finally as the middle square center shape. The middle square center shapes, which are slightly off-center to add a modern touch, appear in nine different sizes. As an option, instructions for the four-color mitered binding are provided. The combination results in a quilt that has color, balance, and movement but is easy to construct.

MATERIALS AND SUPPLIES

Slate, Cactus, **Hibiscus**, Ash, **Hyacinth**,
Jade Green, **Peacock**, **Windsor**,
and Thistle: ¼ yard of each

Snow: 1⅝ yards for background,
sashing, and borders

Binding: ⅜ yard

Backing: 3 yards

Batting: 53″ × 53″

Snow

CUTTING

Slate, Cactus, **Hibiscus**, Ash, **Hyacinth**,
Jade Green, **Peacock**, **Windsor**,
and Thistle:

Cut 1 strip 4″ × width of fabric (WOF)
from each fabric; subcut into 5 squares
4″ × 4″. Cut the remaining rectangle
(4″ × about 20″) into 2 strips 2″ × 20″ each.

Trim 1 square 4″ × 4″ of each color into one
of the following sizes (each color will have
a different size), for 9 block centers:

      1½″ × 1½″

      1½″ × 2″

      1½″ × 2½″

      2″ × 2″

      2″ × 2½″

      2″ × 3″

      2½″ × 2½″

      2½″ × 3″

      3″ × 3″

Snow:
Cut 4 strips 4″ × WOF; subcut into
36 squares 4″ × 4″ for blocks.

Cut 2 strips 3″ × WOF; subcut into
6 rectangles 3″ × 11″ for vertical sashing.

Cut 2 strips 3″ × WOF for horizontal sashing.

Cut 5 strips 4½″ × WOF for borders.

Binding:
Cut 5 strips 2½″ × WOF for double-fold binding.*

*The quilt featured has a four-color
mitered binding. See the instructions
on page 72 for those requirements.*

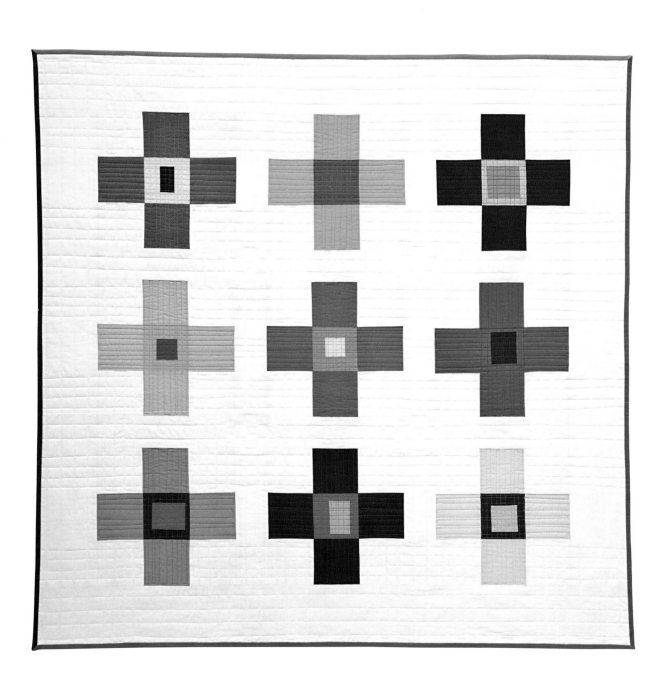

INSTRUCTIONS

All seam allowances are ¼″. Press seam allowances open except where noted.

Block assembly

1. For each of the 9 blocks, make a stack containing 4 squares 4″ × 4″ of a solid fabric, 2 strips 2″ × 20″ of a second solid fabric, 1 small block center of a third solid fabric, and 4 squares 4″ × 4″ of the background fabric.

2. To make the block center, sew a 2″ × 20″ strip to each side of a small solid fabric rectangle center. Press seams toward the block center. Trim the strips even with the edges, and sew the leftover strips to the other 2 sides. Press seams toward the block center.

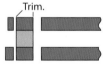

3. Square up the unit to 4″ × 4″. Vary the amount you trim on each side so that some block centers are slightly off-center as shown.

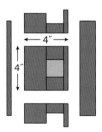

4. Sew a 4″ × 4″ solid fabric square to each side of the block center unit.

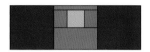

5. Sew a 4″ × 4″ background fabric square to each side of a 4″ × 4″ solid fabric square. Repeat with the remaining 4″ × 4″ solid fabric square and 2 background squares 4″ × 4″.

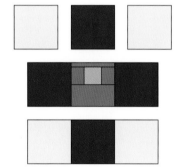

6. Sew the block units together, matching intersecting seams.

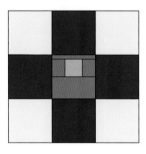

7. Repeat Steps 2 through 6 to make a total of 9 blocks.

Quilt top assembly

1. Refer to the quilt assembly diagram to arrange the blocks on a design wall or flat surface. Sew the blocks and 3″ × 11″ vertical sashing strips together to create 3 rows.

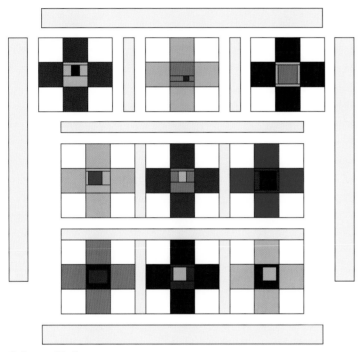

Quilt assembly diagram

2. Sew the 3 rows together with 2 horizontal sashing strips. Trim the sashing strips even with the quilt top edge.

3. Sew 1 border strip to each side of the quilt top. Trim the border strips even with the quilt top and bottom edges.

4. Cut 1 border strip 4½″ × WOF in half. Sew a half to each of the 2 remaining border strips. Sew the border strips to the top and bottom of the quilt top. Trim the borders even with the side quilt edges.

Four-Color Mitered Binding

1. Join on the bias 2 binding strips 2½″ × WOF of the same color, and trim to 2½″ × 49″. Fold in half lengthwise with wrong sides together and press. Repeat for all 4 colors.

2. Sew a binding strip to each of the 4 sides of the quilt top in the following manner: Leaving the first 2″ of the binding strip unattached, begin stitching ¼″ from the corner of the quilt top and stop ¼″ before you reach the next corner. Backstitch to secure at each corner. Repeat to add a binding strip in a different color to each side of the quilt.

3. Fold Binding 2 back on top of itself so raw edges are even. Lay Binding 1 flat so the extra 2″ length extends beyond the edge of the quilt.

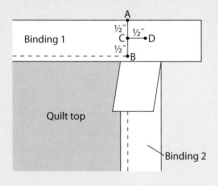

4. Use a ruler to draw a line from the folded edge of Binding 1 (A) to the end of the stitching line of Binding 1 (B), approximately 1″. Mark the center point (C) of Line AB.

5. Draw a ½″ perpendicular line that begins at C and ends at D.

6. Fold the quilt diagonally and pull out both binding ends, matching folded edges, with Binding 1 on top. Stitch from A to D, pivot, and continue sewing from D to B. Trim sthe eam allowance close to the stitching.

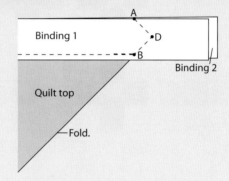

7. Repeat Steps 3–6 to miter the remaining corners.

8. Turn the mitered corners right side out and wrap the binding to the back of the quilt. The folded binding edge will encase the seam allowance and align with the stitching line. Stitch binding in place by hand or machine.

Quilting and finishing

1. Mark quilting designs on the quilt top or plan to stitch without marking.

2. Use your preferred method or refer to Quiltmaking Basics (page 135) to layer and baste the quilt top, batting, and backing.

3. Quilt as desired by hand or machine. My quilt features a grid of stitching with the cross motif echoed in the spaces between the crosses.

4. Refer to Quiltmaking Basics, use your preferred method, or use the four-color mitered binding method (page 72) to bind the quilt.

NICOLA

ORBIT

Designed and made by Jennifer Sampou and machine quilted by Angela Walters

This dramatic quilt was created using an organic, improvisational technique—cutting strips and circles freehand from a spectrum of colors selected on the fly. The rich hues of the fabrics in the circle, placed off-center to eye-catching effect, really pop against the soft background colors. The result is painterly and totally modern.

Special thanks to my quilting friend Teresa Leon—I couldn't have done this project without her!

MATERIALS AND SUPPLIES

Snow, Natural, Celery, **Bone**, **Eggshell**,
Cream, **Sand**, Tan, Champagne, **Ivory**,
Meringue, **Maize**, **Butter**, Mustard, **Light
Parfait**, **Pale Flesh**, Ash, Khaki, Straw, Flesh:
¼ yard each of 10–15 colors for background

Mahogany, **Mocha**, **Spice**, **Herb**, Amber, School Bus,
Apricot, Papaya, Curry, Sunflower, **Pomegranate**, Coral,
Azure, **Ice Frappe**, Cloud, Seafoam, Zucchini, Parsley,
Stone, Cheddar, **Earth**, Taupe:
1 yard each of 15–20 colors for circle appliqué

Snow	Natural	Celery	Bone
Eggshell	Cream	Sand	Tan
Champagne	Ivory	Meringue	Maize
Butter	Mustard	Light Parfait	Pale Flesh
Ash	Khaki	Straw	Flesh

Mahogany	Mocha	Spice	Herb
Amber	School Bus	Apricot	Papaya
Curry	Sunflower	Pomegranate	Coral
Azure	Ice Frappe	Cloud	Seafoam
Zucchini	Parsley	Stone	Cheddar
Earth	Taupe		

NOTE

For the quilt background, choose 10–15
cream and neutral fabrics of very light
values and soft hues. For the circle
appliqués, use a mix of about 15–20 fabrics—mostly brights and saturated colors
mixed with some of the light colors, such
as white, cream, and soft gray, that are in
the background. The mixing helps to give
contrast, depth, and space in the circles. In
my quilt, I ended up using 14 background
colors and 18 bright colors.

Binding: ⅜ yard

Backing: 1⅜ yards

Batting: 45″ × 45″

Freezer paper: 30″ × 30″

Fabric glue stick

INSTRUCTIONS

All seam allowances are approximately ¼˝.

This is not a project of perfect lines and circles. All the pieces for this quilt are cut freehand with a rotary cutter. I like freehand cutting because it's really fast and organic, and I wanted the whole quilt to have a painted effect.

Background assembly

1. From assorted colors, cut approximately 50 background strips in various widths, from 1˝–5˝ × WOF. Do not use a ruler; just cut relatively straight lines with a few gentle curves using a rotary cutter.

2. Begin by placing 2 strips right sides together and stitching them on the machine (no pins needed). Sew some of the seams at a slight angle. Continue adding pieces to create a section about 7˝–10˝ wide. Press as you go. Make 4 or 5 sections.

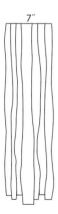

7˝

3. When you have all the sections finished, lay them out in an arrangement you like.

4. Join sections with a strip 2˝–3˝ × WOF. Follow the instructions given in Piecing Gentle Curves (page 50) to sew the

strip to a side of the first section. Repeat to join the strip to the second section.

5. Repeat Step 4 until you have a full square approximately 44˝ × 44˝. It's okay to have uneven ends; you will trim them later. Press well with steam.

Circle appliqué assembly

For the circle appliqués, I made a base of rings from neutral colors, then added brights and darks in arcs and full circles. Cut out circles in graduated sizes, beginning with the largest circle base, and then cut the rings from those circles.

1. Select 5 or 6 soft, neutral fabrics in a pleasing rotation of color to form the circle base. In my quilt, the base colors are 2 greens, a tan, a midbrown, and an off-white.

2. To make a circle template, attach a string to a pencil. Pin the other end of the string to the middle of a piece of freezer paper, and draw the outer circle. I used a string approximately 14˝ long for my outer circle. Draw another circle 1½˝ inside the outer circle. Continue drawing circles inside circles until you have 5 or 6 rings.

3. Cut out the 5 or 6 freezer paper rings and iron a ring onto each of the base circle fabrics. Cut out each of the rings freehand, adding at least a 1˝ overlap to each edge of the freezer paper ring. Do not be exact when cutting. Varying the widths of the rings will make your design interesting and organic.

Cut.

Freezer paper ring

4. Layer the rings on top of each other, with the largest ring on the bottom and the smallest ring on the top.

5. Begin to "paint" on top of the base of rings with the bright and saturated color fabrics. These give life to the circle appliqué. Have fun with the brights and darks, of which you only need a little bit. Cut arcs or full circles free-hand and arrange them on the base rings.

6. Lay all of the raw-edged rings on top of the assembled background, and baste or use a fabric glue stick to attach them temporarily. Make sure all the pieces are very secure so they do not move when you stitch them down. You can play with the position of the ring on the background. I pre-ferred mine off-center and in the upper left-hand corner. I also liked the aesthetic of cutting off part of the ring on the top and left side. I stitched my rings down during the quilting process, but you can do some appliqué stitching now if you prefer.

7. Trim the quilt top to the desired size.

Quilting and finishing

1. Use your favorite method or refer to Quiltmaking Basics (page 135) to layer and baste the quilt top, batting, and backing.

2. If you use free-motion quilting, you will find that raw edges happen, and little bits of the ends may fray off. Don't worry; it's an organic process. Enjoy the development and the jux-taposition of the raw-edged motion of the circle on the clean, quiet pieced background. You can keep adding or subtracting as you go. In the end you will have a quilt that is unique to you. Have fun with the creative process.

3. Use your favorite method or refer to Quiltmaking Basics to bind the quilt.

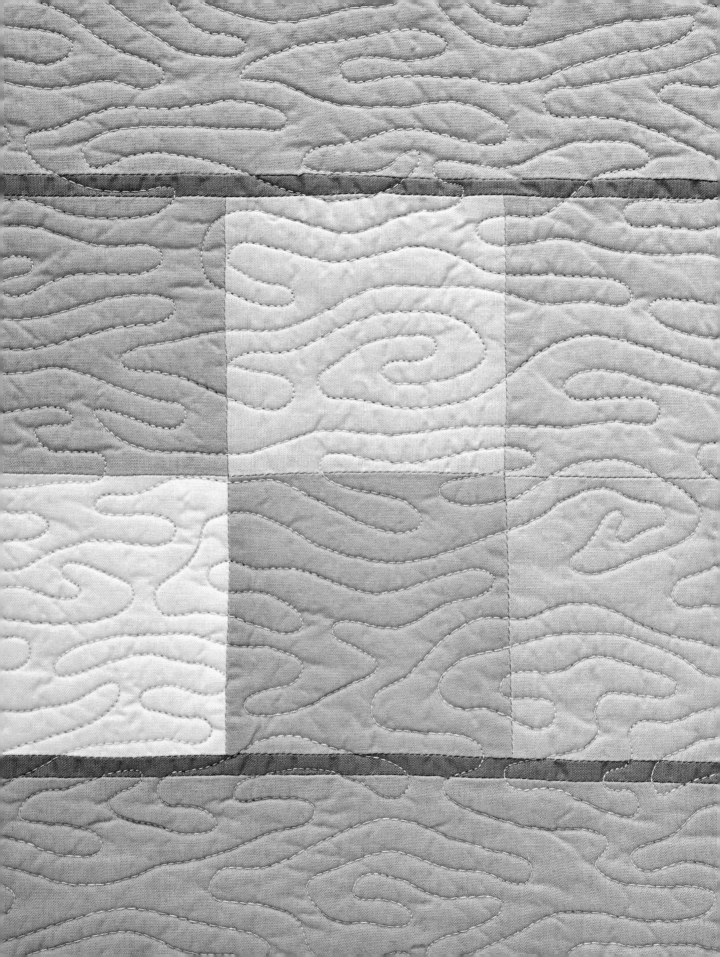

SANIBEL

Designed and made by Modern Quilt Studio
— Weeks Ringle and Bill Kerr —

Finished quilt size: 50¼″ × 80½″

When we were invited to design a project for this book using Kona Cotton Solids, we wanted to highlight the best aspect of the line, which is the vast array of colors. We immediately began working on designs with subtle color work that would not be possible with fewer colors.

The colors of the seashore came to mind. Although many travelers to the sea focus on the beauty of the water, it was the interplay among the soft colors of the shore that was of particular interest to us. The rich greens of the seaweed contrast so beautifully with the soft pinks and peaches of the seashells.

It seems as if there are too many shades of beige and cream and sage to count. So as we looked at the Kona Cotton Color Card; that's what we wanted to capture.

We also wanted to design a quilt that is nontraditional in structure, suggesting that there are no limitations to what you can do with solids. Just as the Amish quilts made with solids look fresh and modern 100 years later, so will the quilts in this book. Note also the contrasting texture of the quilting. Unlike prints, which sometimes compete for attention with quilting, solids allow your stitches to show and add an additional layer of visual interest.

MATERIALS AND SUPPLIES

Parsley: 2 yards for background

10 assorted pink **and** peach **fabrics:** ½ yard total* (We used a single 1½″ × 44″ strip each of Flesh, Light Parfait, Peach, Petal, Primrose, Pink, Dusty Peach, Ice Peach, Baby Pink, and Peony.)

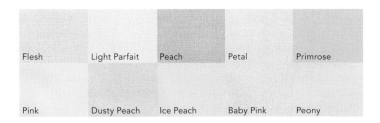

Flesh · Light Parfait · Peach · Petal · Primrose

Pink · Dusty Peach · Ice Peach · Baby Pink · Peony

14 assorted greens, cream, **and** tan **fabrics:** 2 yards total** (We used a single 4″ × 44″ strip each of Eggshell, Celery, Butter, Raffia, Tarragon, Cream, Seafoam, Ivory, Honey Dew, Artichoke, Meringue, Khaki, Green Tea, and Champagne.)

Eggshell · Celery · Butter · Raffia · Tarragon

Cream · Seafoam · Ivory · Honey Dew · Artichoke

Meringue · Khaki · Green Tea · Champange · Parsley

Herb

Herb: ¾ yard for frame/accent strips

Binding: ⅝ yard

Backing: 3⅝ yards

Batting: 58″ × 88″

Kaufman Kona Cottons are 44″ wide. If using a narrower fabric, you will need more yardage.

** *Although only 1¾ yards are actually needed, we recommend buying more for the sake of easier cutting.*

CUTTING

Parsley:

Cut 5 pieces 4½″ × 35¾″.

Cut 2 pieces 8″ × 35¾″.

Cut 14 strips 2¾″ × 15″.

Cut 14 pieces 4½″ × 7″.

Assorted pinks **and** peaches:

Cut 1 strip 1½″ × 44″. Subcut into 3 strips 1½″ × 14″. Repeat for each of 10 colors, for a total of 30 strips.

Assorted greens, creams, **and** tans:

Cut 1 strip 4″ × 44″; subcut into 9 squares 4″ × 4″. Repeat for each of 14 colors, for a total of 126 squares.

Herb:

Cut 6 strips 1″ × 15″.

Cut 6 strips ¾″ × 7½″.

Cut 12 strips ¾″ × 35¾″.

Cut 14 strips ¾″ × 6½″.

Cut 14 strips ¾″ × 7″.

Binding:

Cut 8 strips 2″ × width of fabric.

INSTRUCTIONS

Making the peach/ pink squares

1. Sew together the long sides of 3 assorted 1½″ × 14″ pink and peach strips. Press the seams open. Repeat for all the remaining 1½″ × 14″ pink and peach strips.

2. Crosscut each strip set into 9 units 1½″ × 3½″.

3. Sew the short ends of 2 units 1½″ × 3½″ together to make a row. Press the seams open. Repeat for all the remaining pieces. You'll be making a couple more sets than you need, but this will make for easier layout later.

Join 2 units to make a row.

4. Lay out 6 rows; check for even distribution of colors. Number the rows to keep them in order.

5. Sew the first 2 rows together, pinning through the seams to align the corners. Press the seams open. Continue joining the other rows until you have a full square of 6 rows completed.

Join 6 rows to make a square.

6. Repeat Steps 3–5 to make 7 squares.

7. Sew ¾″ × 6½″ Herb strips to the left and right sides of each pink/peach square set;

press the seams open. Sew ¾″ × 7″ Herb strips to the top and bottom of each pink/ peach square set. Press the seams open.

Making the tan/ cream/green sets

1. Sew together all the assorted 4″ × 4″ squares into pairs. Press the seams open. You'll be making a couple more pairs than you need, but this will make for easier layout later.

2. Lay out 10 of the pairs side by side as shown, checking for even distribution of colors. Pin carefully to align the seams, and sew the pairs together. Press the seams open. Repeat to make a total of 6 sets of 20 squares.

3. Sew a ¾″ × 7½″ Herb strip to the right-hand side of each tan/cream/green square set; press the seams open. Sew ¾″ × 35¾″ Herb strips to the top and bottom of each tan/cream/ green square set; press the seams open.

Quilt assembly

1. Sew a 4½″ × 7″ Parsley piece to both sides of each pink/peach/Herb square set; press the seams open. Sew a 2¾″ × 15″ Parsley piece to the top and bottom of each pink/peach/Herb square set. Press the seams open. Make 7.

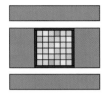

2. The quilt goes together in 2 columns. Refer to the quilt assembly diagram to make the right-hand column by sewing a 1″ × 15″ Herb strip between each pair of the Parsley/pink/peach blocks from Step 1. Press the seams open.

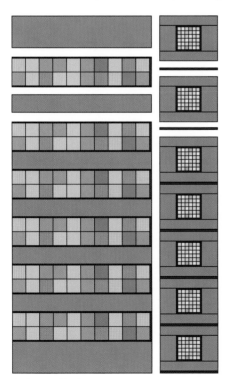

Quilt assembly diagram

3. Assemble the left-hand column, sewing a 35¾″ × 8″ Parsley strip to the topmost and bottommost tan/cream/green sets, and a 35¾″ × 4½″ Parsley strip between the others. Press the seams open.

4. Pin the left and right columns together so that the Herb strips in the right column meet the centers of the tan/cream/green square sets. Sew and press the seams open.

Quilting and finishing

1. Mark your quilting design on the quilt top, or plan to quilt without marking.

2. Use your favorite method or refer to Quiltmaking Basics (page 135) to layer and baste the quilt top, batting, and backing.

3. Quilt as desired. We used an allover pattern that gives the quilt subtle texture.

4. Use your favorite method or refer to Quiltmaking Basics to bind the quilt.

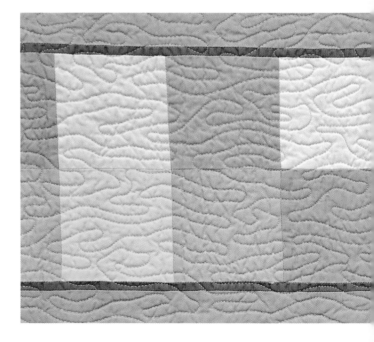

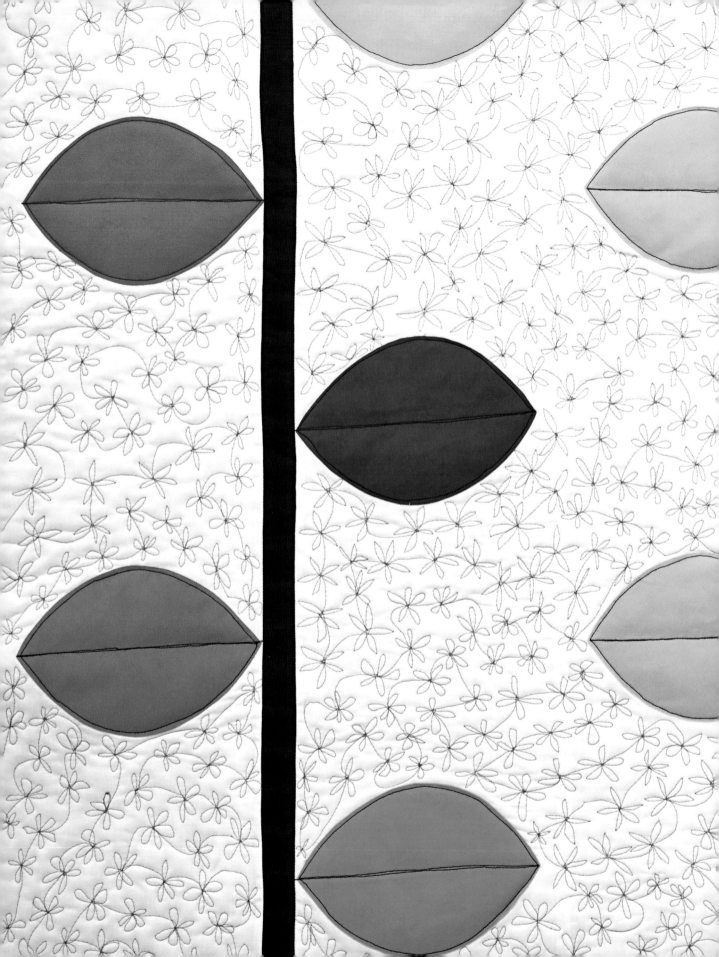

SPRING WILL COME

Designed and made by Kajsa Wikman

Finished quilt size: 54½″ × 90″

If there is not a hint of optimism in a quilt, it is not my quilt! The dreadfully long and dark winters in Finland, where I live, call for color and light. This quilt was designed in the middle of winter when the snow had turned dirty and gray, but the sun gave promise of spring. I chose gray thread for my quilting to symbolically turn the dirty slosh into something pretty!

The only traditional piecing I used for the quilt is in the black stems and the white background, so the quilt is fairly easy to piece. The appliqué is raw-edge, and instead of embroidering the text, I decided to turn the words into appliqué pieces. I am very content with the cut paper look of it!

If you are looking for a more graphic, less whimsical look, why not remove the bird and the text and continue the stems all the way up? Use gray for the background and straight-line quilting.

MATERIALS AND SUPPLIES

Bleach White:* 5⅛ yards for the quilt top and binding

Charcoal: ⅝ yard for the stems and text

Bleach White*   Charcoal

Candy Pink, Carnation, **Chartreuse, Sour Apple,** Robin Egg, **Peacock, Candy Green, Lupine, Lapis,** Lemon, **Tangerine, Lime,** Canary, Papaya: ¼ yard each for leaf and bird appliqués

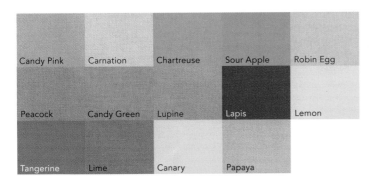

Candy Pink	Carnation	Chartreuse	Sour Apple	Robin Egg
Peacock	Candy Green	Lupine	Lapis	Lemon
Tangerine	Lime	Canary	Papaya	

Backing: 5⅝ yards

Batting: 63″ × 98″

Paper-backed fusible web (17″ wide): 3¼ yards

White sewing thread

Medium gray machine quilting thread

Black machine quilting thread

Masking tape

CUTTING

Bleach White:

Cut 6 strips *lengthwise* 9″ × 90″.

Cut 3 strips *lengthwise* 1½″ × 13½″.

Cut 4 strips 2¼″ × 90″ for double-fold binding.

Cut 12 strips 1¼″ × 2¼″ for binding stripes.

Charcoal:

Cut 6 strips 1½″ × width of fabric (WOF) for stems.

Cut 15 strips 1¼″ × 2¼″ for binding stripes.

*NOTE

The maufacturer suggests using White Kona Cotton Solid instead of Bleach White because White has the same finishing as other colors, which makes it more resistant to picking up release dyes from other fabrics.

INSTRUCTIONS

Note: All seam allowances are ¼″.

Appliqué

Appliqué patterns are on pages 92 and 93.

1. Enlarge and trace the appliqué pieces with a pencil onto the paper side of the fusible web. Cut out, adding a ¼″ around each piece.

2. Follow the manufacturer's instructions to fuse the pattern pieces onto the fabrics as follows:

Candy Green: 1 bird body, 3 leaves

Candy Pink: 1 bird tail, 2 leaves

Lapis: 1 bird wing, 3 leaves

Papaya: 1 beak, 2 leaves

Tangerine: 3 leaves

Lime: 3 leaves

Carnation, Chartreuse, Sour Apple, Robin Egg, Peacock, Lupine, Lemon, Canary: 2 leaves each

Charcoal: text, 1 bird's eye, 2 legs

3. Use sharp scissors to cut out the appliqué pieces on the drawn lines.

Quilt assembly

1. Piece 2 Charcoal strips 1½″ × WOF together end to end and trim to 1½″ × 77″. Make 3.

2. Sew a 1½″ × 77″ Charcoal strip and a 1½″ × 13½″ Bleach White strip end to end. Press the seams open. Repeat to make 3 stems.

3. Refer to the quilt assembly diagram to sew together the 9″ × 90″ Bleach White strips and the 1½″ × 90″ stem strips. Press the seams open.

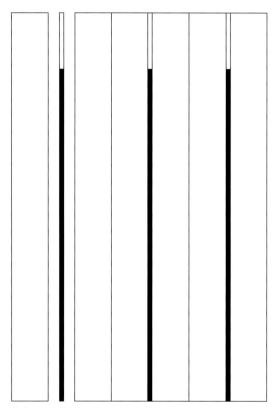

Quilt assembly diagram

4. Peel the paper off the appliqué pieces and lay out the quilt top on a flat surface. Refer to the quilt photo (page 89) to place the bird on top of the left stem. The pieces with an overlap allowance (indicated by a dashed line on the template pattern) go underneath. Press to fuse into place.

5. Place the text appliqué pieces on the quilt 5″–6″ from the top edge, using the photo (page 89) as reference.

6. Starting from the top, arrange the leaves along the stems 7″ apart. The lowest leaves should be about 5″ from the bottom edge. Use masking tape to keep the leaves temporarily in place. Fuse into place.

Making striped binding

1. Sew 4 of the 1¼″ × 2¼″ White binding strips to 5 of the 1¼″ × 2¼″ Charcoal binding strips, alternating colors as shown. Press seams open. Make 3 pieced units.

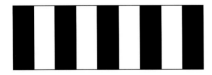

2. Join the 2¼″ × 90″ White binding strips end to end, inserting a striped pieced unit from Step 1 in each seam.

3. Press the binding strip in half lengthwise with wrong sides together to form a double-fold binding.

Quilting and finishing

1. Mark your quilting design on the quilt top, or plan to quilt without marking.

2. Use your favorite method or refer to Quiltmaking Basics (page 135) to layer and baste the quilt top, batting, and backing.

3. With black thread in your sewing machine, appliqué the stems and leaves through all the layers with a straight stitch. Stitch ⅛″ from the edges.

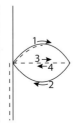

TEMPLATES

4. Stitch the bird in place, stitching back and forth on the tail to make "feathers."

5. Carefully appliqué the text into place.

6. Using a darning foot and with the machine's feed dogs dropped, quilt a flower pattern using the gray thread.

7. Refer to Quiltmaking Basics (page 135) to bind the quilt using double-fold binding.

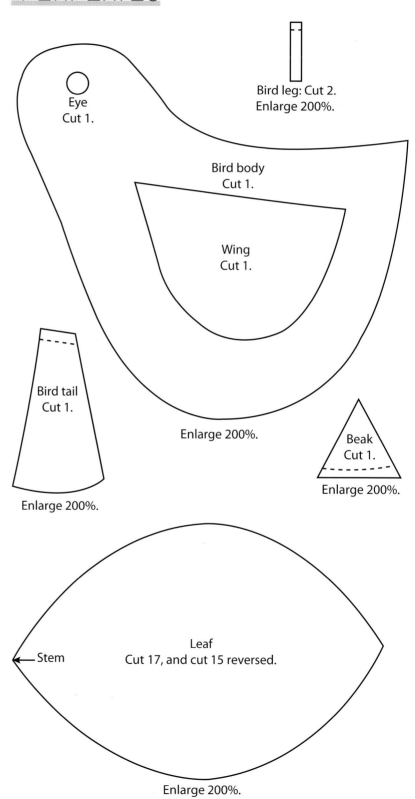

Bird leg: Cut 2.
Enlarge 200%.

Eye
Cut 1.

Bird body
Cut 1.

Wing
Cut 1.

Bird tail
Cut 1.

Enlarge 200%.

Enlarge 200%.

Beak
Cut 1.

Enlarge 200%.

Stem

Leaf
Cut 17, and cut 15 reversed.

Enlarge 200%.

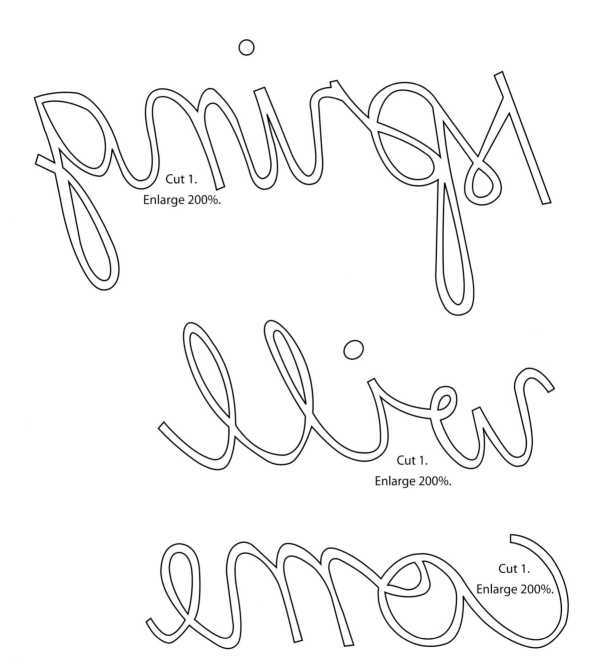

Cut 1.
Enlarge 200%.

Cut 1.
Enlarge 200%.

Cut 1.
Enlarge 200%.

STACKED BLANKETS

Designed and made by Valori Wells

Finished quilt size: 50½″ × 65½″

A photograph of beautiful hand-dyed and quilted blankets on shelves inspired this quilt. I loved the layers of color and the simple lines that were created by the folded blankets.

To make this quilt, you will use intuitive piecing—cutting without rulers to create your own unique, gently curved and angled shapes. Choosing from a palette of all solid fabric allows you to play with value and contrast among your core and accent colors.

MATERIALS AND SUPPLIES

> ### NOTE
>
> You do not have to use the exact colors shown in my quilt. When choosing your colors, select nine core colors and five more intense accent colors. For the vertical accent strip, choose a dark-value color.

Coal, **Paprika**, Apricot, Ash, **Copen**, Bahama Blue, **Tan**, **Wheat**, Primrose, **Stone**, **Peridot**, **Lime**, **Yarrow**, Sunflower: ⅝ yard each of 9 core colors and 5 accent colors for the panels

Medium Grey: ¼ yard for the dark accent strips

Backing: ½ yard*

Binding: ⅝ yard

Batting: 59˝ × 74˝

*Combine with leftover fabric from the core and accent colors to piece the quilt back.

CUTTING

9 core colors:
Cut each into approximately 10 pieces 4˝ × 16½˝ for a total of 90 pieces.

5 accent colors:
Cut each into approximately 10 pieces 4˝ × 16½˝ for a total of 50 pieces.

Dark accent color:
Cut 3 strips 1½˝ × 44˝.* Sew into 1 long strip; subcut into 2 strips 1½˝ × 65½˝.

If your fabric is less than 44˝ wide, cut 4 strips and piece together end to end. Then subcut to get 2 strips 1½˝ × 65½˝.

Binding:
Cut 7 strips 2½˝ × 40˝.

> ### NOTE
>
> After cutting the initial strips for the panels, you will put away your ruler and cut intuitively. This will create simple curves and slight angles to the piecing. The general rule that I used was to keep the accent colors in narrower strips than the core colors.

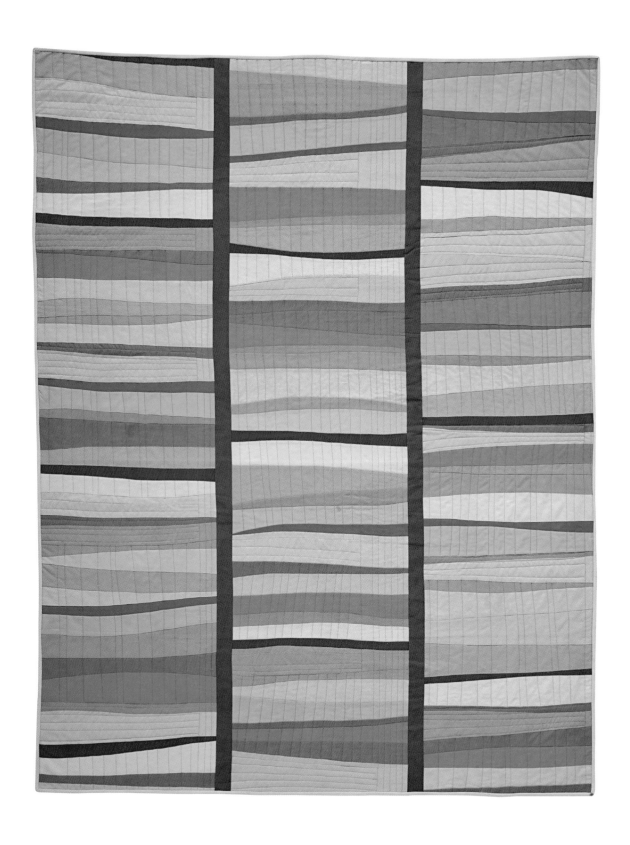

INSTRUCTIONS

Piecing the quilt top

This quilt has 3 vertical panels, each approximately 16½″ wide, divided by 2 dark vertical accent strips.

1. To piece a panel, pick 2 different fabric pieces 4″ × 16½″, and lay the first on top of the second, overlapping by approximately 1½″. Follow the instructions in Piecing Gentle Curves (page 50) to connect the 2 pieces in an organic fashion. Once you do a few of them, you will find a rhythm to the piecing. The ends may be a little uneven, but you can trim them later.

2. Press the sewn pieces, and lay the unit down again to repeat the cutting process. Press after sewing each seam.

3. As you cut pieces, vary the widths (overlaps) among the accent colors and core colors to create a rhythm of value and line contrasts.

> ## NOTE
>
> Every four or five pieces, check to make sure the panel measures at least 16½″ wide. This will help keep it straight. Lining up the stitched partial panel with the next piece of fabric on the grid line of a cutting mat also will help you keep the panel straight.

4. Continue cutting and stitching pieces until the panel measures at least 65½″ long. Trim the panel to 16½″ × 65½″.

5. Repeat Steps 1–4 to make 3 panels.

6. Sew the first panel to the 1½″ × 65½″ dark accent strip; press. Sew on the center panel, an accent strip, and finally the third panel.

Quilting and finishing

1. Creatively piece the remaining quilt top fabrics and the backing fabric to form a backing 59″ × 74″.

Quilt back

2. Mark quilting designs on the quilt top or plan to stitch without marking.

3. Use your preferred method or refer to Quiltmaking Basics (page 135) to layer and baste the quilt top, batting, and backing.

4. Quilt as desired by hand or machine. I quilted both vertical and horizontal lines to accent the piecing.

5. Refer to Quiltmaking Basics, or use your preferred method to bind the quilt.

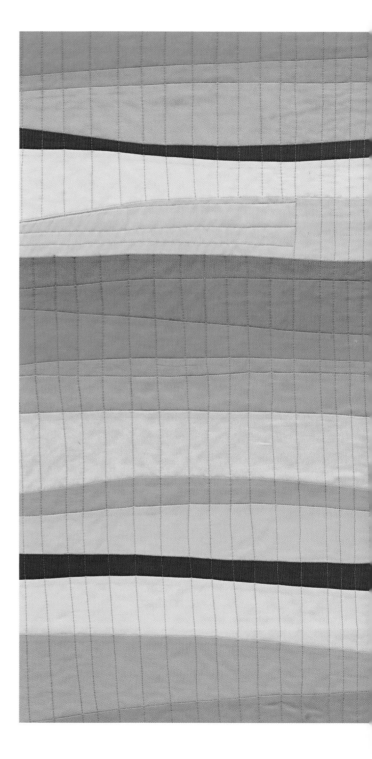

STEPPING STONES

Designed and made by Lisa Call

Finished block size: various, **Finished quilt size:** 60½˝ × 40½˝

This quilt design was inspired by a pattern of stones set into the floor of an outdoor yoga studio in Costa Rica. The colors are taken from the surrounding landscape—the blues of the sea, the greens of the jungle, and the browns of the earth.

The quilt block features a large square surrounded by a number of smaller contrasting squares, with strips of background "mortar" set between them. Several different sizes and variations of this block are used within the quilt. Some of the blocks are surrounded on all sides by the background, while neighboring "stepping stones" overlap others.

Although there are many small pieces in this quilt, it goes together quickly because it is made up of squares and rectangles. A bit of strip piecing speeds up the process of creating the rows of smaller "stones" that surround the larger centers.

The use of the richly colored Kona Cotton Solids results in a bold graphic design and provides a canvas for intricate quilting lines to set off the design.

MATERIALS AND SUPPLIES

For some fabrics, you can use scraps
that are large enough to cut into squares
in the dimensions indicated.

Slate: 2¼ yards for background and binding

Asparagus: 1 square 7½˝ × 7½˝ for Section A

Stone: ⅛ yard for Section A

Champagne: 1 square 4½˝ × 4½˝ for Section A

Olive: ⅛ yard for Section A

Zucchini: 1 square 4½˝ × 4½˝ for Section A

Candy Blue: ⅛ yard for Section A

Seafoam: 1 fat quarter or 1 square
13½˝ × 13½˝ for Section B

Blue Bell: ¼ yard for Section B

Khaki: 1 square 4½˝ × 4½˝ for Section C

Aqua: ⅛ yard for Section C

Celery: 1 square 4½˝ × 4½˝ for Section C

Regatta: ⅛ yard for Section C

Lake: 1 square 4½˝ × 4½˝ for Section C

Ash: ⅛ yard for Section C

Denim: 1 fat quarter or 1 square
13½˝ × 13½˝ for Section D

Eggshell: ¼ yard for Section D

Robin Egg: 1 square 7½˝ × 7½˝ for Section E

Sage: ⅛ yard for Section E

Artichoke: 1 square 8½˝ × 8½˝ for Section F

Taupe: ⅛ yard for Section F

Light Parfait: 1 square 8½˝ × 8½˝ for Section G

Green Tea: ¼ yard for Sections C, F, and G

Backing: 3 yards

Batting: 48˝ × 68˝

NOTE

This quilt is constructed in seven sections, A–G.

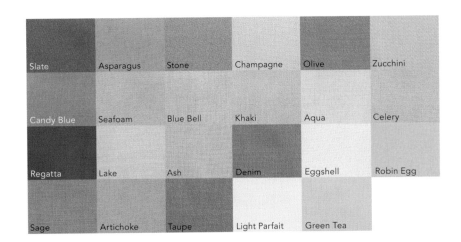

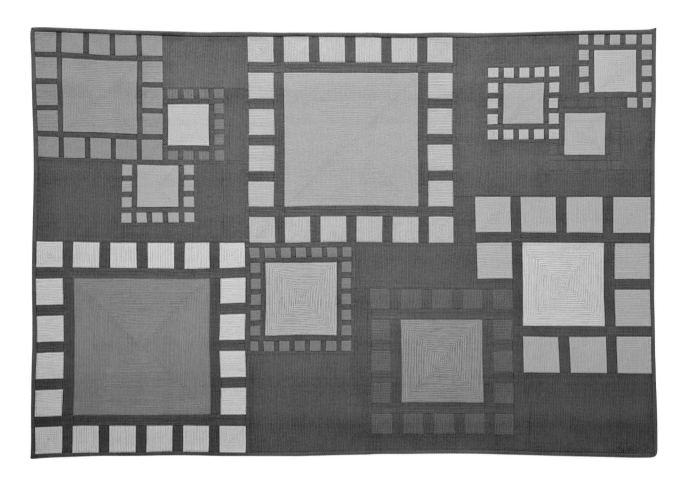

CUTTING

For the background fabric (Slate), make the basic cuts indicated below. Refer to the individual cutting charts for Sections A–G to subcut the Slate strips and to cut the other fabrics. If you prefer to cut all pieces of each fabric at once, be sure to group and label them for Sections A–G.

Slate:
Cut the following 1″-wide and 1½″-wide basic strips first; then cut the binding strips. Use the remaining fabric for the background pieces as indicated in each section.

Cut 10 basic strips 1″ × width of fabric (WOF).

Cut 10 basic strips 1½″ × WOF.

Binding:
Cut 6 strips 2½″ × WOF for double-fold binding.

INSTRUCTIONS

All seam allowances are ¼˝. Press all seams toward the Slate background fabric.

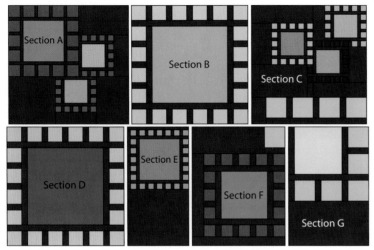

Quilt assembly diagram

> ## NOTE
>
> To avoid mixing up pieces from different sections, during cutting and construction, place all cut fabric pieces on a design wall or flat surface, and refer to the assembly diagrams for placement.

Basic block assembly

Use these general instructions for making the blocks. Note that the blocks in this quilt vary in the size of the squares, divider strips, and number of surrounding squares. That information will be specified in each section.

Some blocks are overlapped by others, so they are not complete blocks. The Green Tea/Light Parfait block is constructed in sections. Detailed instructions for these cases are noted in the instructions for the appropriate sections.

> ## NOTE
>
> Piecing with an accurate ¼˝ seam allowance is required to create evenly sized squares.

1. To create the strips of small squares that surround the block centers, stitch a strip of fabric for the small squares to a divider strip of Slate background fabric, and press. Subcut it into the specified number of pieces.

2. Stitch pieces from Step 1 together, oriented as shown below; add a final square to the end. This forms a single row of surrounding squares. The top and bottom rows include the corner squares, so they will be longer than the rows for the right and left sides.

3. Stitch a narrow Slate divider strip to the long edge of the row of squares.

4. Sew the right and left rows of surrounding squares to the center square. Then sew on the top and bottom rows of surrounding squares.

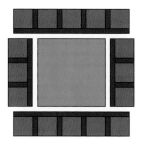

Section A

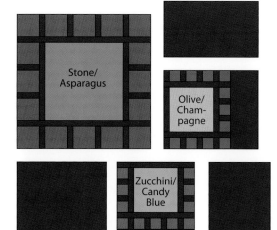

Section A assembly diagram

This section is made up of 3 blocks: Stone/Asparagus, Olive/Champagne (partial block), and Candy Blue/Zucchini (partial block).

SECTION A CUTTING CHART

FABRIC	QUANTITY	SIZE
Slate (subcut from basic strips)	1	1″ × 30″
	2	1″ × 12½″
	4	1″ × 7½″
	1	1″ × 15″
	2	1″ × 6½″
	4	1″ × 4½″
	1	1″ × 12″
Slate (cut from remaining yardage)	1	3″ × 7½″
	1	5½″ × 9″
	1	2½″ × 7½″
	1	6″ × 8½″
	1	8½″ × 8½″
Asparagus	1	7½″ × 7½″
Stone	1	2½″ × 30″
	4	2½″ × 2½″
Champagne	1	4½″ × 4½″
Olive	1	1½″ × 15″
	1	1½″ × 1½″
Zucchini	1	4½″ × 4½″
Candy Blue	1	1½″ × 12″
	3	1½″ × 1½″

Stone/Asparagus block

1. Stitch the 2½″ × 30″ Stone strip to the 1″ × 30″ Slate divider strip; press. Subcut into 12 pieces 2½″ wide.

2. Stitch 4 pieces from Step 1 together plus a final Stone square 2½″ × 2½″ for the top row. Repeat for the bottom row. Stitch a 1″ × 12½″ Slate divider strip to each row.

3. Stitch together 2 pieces from Step 1 plus a final Stone square 2½″ × 2½″ for the left row. Repeat for the right row. Stitch a 1″ × 7½″ Slate divider strip to each row.

4. Stitch the rows from Step 3 to either side of the 7½″ × 7½″ Asparagus square. Sew the rows from Step 2 to the top and bottom to complete the Stone/Asparagus block.

Olive/Champagne
partial block

1. Stitch the 1½″ × 15″ Olive strip to the 1″ × 15″ Slate divider strip; press. Subcut into 10 pieces 1½″ wide.

2. Stitch together 4 pieces from Step 1 (with no final square) for the top row. Repeat for the bottom row. Position the rows so that the Olive square is to the far right. Stitch a 1″ × 6½″ Slate divider strip to the top of one row and bottom of another row.

3. Stitch together 2 pieces from Step 1 plus a final Olive square 1½″ × 1½″ for the right row. Stitch a 1″ × 4½″ Slate divider strip to the row.

4. Stitch the row from Step 3 to the right-hand side of the 4½″ × 4½″ Champagne square. Instead of a row of squares, stitch a 1″ × 4½″ Slate divider strip to the left side of the square. Sew the rows from Step 2 to the top and bottom of the Champagne unit.

Candy Blue/Zucchini
partial block

1. Stitch the 1½″ × 12″ Candy Blue strip to the 1″ × 12″ Slate divider strip; press. Subcut into 8 pieces 1½″ wide.

2. Stitch 4 pieces from Step 1 together plus a final Candy Blue square 1½″ × 1½″ for the bottom row. Stitch a 1″ × 7½″ Slate divider strip to the row.

3. Stitch 2 pieces from Step 1 together plus a final Candy Blue square 1½″ × 1½″ for the left row. Repeat for the right row. Stitch a 1″ × 4½″ Slate divider strip to each of the rows.

4. Stitch the rows from Step 3 to the left and right sides of the 4½″ × 4½″ Zucchini square. Stitch a 1″ × 7½″ Slate divider strip to the top edge of the square. Stitch the row from Step 2 to the bottom to complete the Candy Blue/Zucchini partial block.

Section A assembly

Refer to the Section A assembly diagram (page 105) to arrange the blocks and background pieces on a design wall or flat surface.

1. Sew the 3″ × 7½″ Slate background piece to the right edge of the Olive/Champagne block. Sew the 5½″ × 9″ Slate background piece to the top of the block, and sew the Stone/Asparagus block to the left of the Olive/Champagne block section.

2. Sew the 2½″ × 7½″ Slate background piece to the bottom of the Candy Blue/Zucchini block. Sew the 6″ × 8½″ Slate background piece to the right edge of the block, and sew the 8½″ × 8½″ Slate piece to the left edge.

3. Sew the Candy Blue/Zucchini block section to the bottom edge of the section you assembled in Step 1.

4. The section should measure 21″ wide × 20½″ high.

Section B

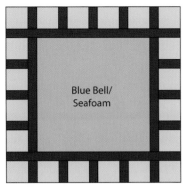

Section B assembly diagram

This section has 1 Blue Bell/Seafoam block.

SECTION B CUTTING CHART

FABRIC	QUANTITY	SIZE
Slate (subcut from basic strips)	1	1½″ × 39″
	1	1½″ × 9″
	2	1½″ × 20½″
	2	1½″ × 13½″
Seafoam	1	13½″ × 13½″
Blue Bell	1	3″ × 39″
	1	3″ × 9″
	4	3″ × 3″

Blue Bell/Seafoam block

1. Stitch the 3″ × 39″ Blue Bell strip to the 1½″ × 39″ Slate divider strip; press. Subcut into 13 pieces 3″ wide. Stitch the 3″ × 9″ Blue Bell strip to the 1½″ × 9″ Slate divider strip; press. Subcut into 3 pieces 3″ wide. You now have 16 identical pieces 3″ × 4″.

2. Stitch together 5 pieces from Step 1 plus a final Blue Bell square 3″ × 3″ for the top row. Repeat for the bottom row. Stitch a 1½″ × 20½″ Slate divider strip to each row.

3. Stitch together 3 pieces from Step 1 plus a final Blue Bell square 3″ × 3″ for the left row. Repeat for the right row. Stitch a 1½″ × 13½″ Slate divider strip to each row.

4. Stitch the rows from Step 3 to the left and right sides of the 13½″ × 13½″ Seafoam square. Stitch the rows from Step 2 to the top and bottom of the block.

5. The section should measure to 20½″ × 20½″.

Section C

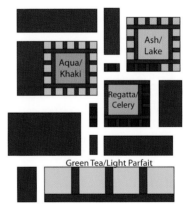

Section C assembly diagram

This section is made up of 4 blocks: Aqua/Khaki, Regatta/Celery (partial block), Ash/Lake, and Green Tea/Light Parfait (partial block).

SECTION C CUTTING CHART

FABRIC	QUANTITY	SIZE
Slate (subcut from basic strips)	1	1″ × 18″
	4	1″ × 7½″
	6	1″ × 4½″
	1	1″ × 16½″
	1	1″ × 1½″
	2	1″ × 6½″
	1	1″ × 15″
	1	1½″ × 12″
	1	1½″ × 17½″
	1	1½″ × 3″
Slate (cut from remaining fabric)	1	4″ × 7½″
	1	3½″ × 11″
	1	6″ × 10″
	1	2½″ × 6½″
	1	3½″ × 6½″
	1	3″ × 9½″
	1	3″ × 5″
Khaki	1	4½″ × 4½″
Aqua	1	1½″ × 18″
	4	1½″ × 1½″
Celery	1	4½″ × 4½″
Regatta	1	1½″ × 16½″
	2	1½″ × 1½″
Lake	1	4½″ × 4½″
Ash	1	1½″ × 15″
	3	1½″ × 1½″
Green Tea	1	4″ × 12″
	1	4″ × 4″

Aqua/Khaki block

1. Stitch the 1½″ × 18″ Aqua strip to the 1″ × 18″ Slate divider strip; press. Subcut into 12 pieces 1½″ wide.

2. Stitch together 4 pieces from Step 1 plus a final Aqua square 1½″ × 1½″ for the top row. Repeat for the bottom row. Stitch a 1″ × 7½″ Slate divider strip to each row.

3. Stitch together 2 pieces from Step 1 plus a final Aqua square 1½″ × 1½″ for the left row. Repeat for the right row. Stitch a 1″ × 4½″ Slate divider strip to each row.

4. Stitch a row from Step 3 to either side of the 4½″ × 4½″ Khaki square. Stitch the rows from Step 2 to the top and bottom of the block.

Regatta/Celery partial block

1. Stitch the 1½″ × 16½″ Regatta strip to the 1″ × 16½″ Slate divider strip; press. Subcut into 11 pieces 1½″ wide.

2. Stitch together 4 pieces from Step 1 (with no final square) for the bottom row. Position the row so that the Regatta square is at the far right; stitch a 1″ × 6½″ Slate divider strip to the top of the row.

3. Stitch together 2 pieces from Step 1 plus a final Regatta square 1½″ × 1½″ for the right row. Stitch a 1″ × 4½″ Slate divider strip to the row.

4. Stitch the row from Step 3 to the right-hand side of the Celery square 4½″ × 4½″. Instead of a row of squares, stitch a 1″ × 4½″ Slate divider strip to the left side of the square, and stitch a 1″ × 6½″ Slate divider strip to the top. Sew the row from Step 2 to the bottom of the block.

5. Stitch 1 piece from Step 1 to the 1″ × 1½″ piece of Slate for a portion of the top row. Set aside to use in Step 3 of the final Section C assembly (page 109).

6. Stitch together 2 pieces from Step 1 plus a final Regatta square 1½″ × 1½″. Set aside to use in Step 3 of the Ash/Lake block (page 109).

7. Stitch together 2 pieces from Step 1 (with no final square) for the left row. Set aside to use in Step 2 of Section C assembly.

Ash/Lake block

1. Stitch the 1½″ × 15″ Ash strip to the 1″ × 15″ Slate divider strip; press. Subcut into 10 pieces 1½″ wide.

2. Stitch together 4 pieces from Step 1 plus a final Ash square 1½″ × 1½″ for the top row. Stitch a 1″ × 7½″ Slate divider strip to the row.

3. Stitch together 2 pieces from Step 1. Stitch the partial row from Step 6 of the Regatta/Celery block to the left of the Ash squares. Position the row with the Ash squares at the far right, and stitch a 1″ × 7½″ Slate divider strip to the top of the row.

4. Stitch together 2 pieces from Step 1 plus a final Ash square 1½″ × 1½″ for the left row. Repeat for the right row. Stitch a 1″ × 4½″ Slate divider strip to a side of each row.

5. Stitch the rows from Step 4 to the left and right sides of the 4½″ × 4½″ Lake square. Stitch the row from Step 2 to the top of the block. Stitch the row from Step 3 to the bottom of the block as shown in the Section C assembly diagram (page 107).

Green Tea/Light Parfait partial block (top row)

1. Stitch the 4″ × 12″ Green Tea strip to the 1½″ × 12″ Slate divider strip; press. Subcut into 3 pieces 4″ wide.

2. Stitch together the 3 pieces plus the final Green Tea square 4″ × 4″ for the top row. Stitch a 1½″ × 17½″ Slate divider strip to the row.

Section C assembly

1. Refer to the Section C assembly diagram to arrange the blocks, the pieces from Steps 5 and 7 of the Regatta/Celery block, and the Slate background pieces.

2. Sew the 4″ × 7½″ Slate background piece to the left side of the Aqua/Khaki block, and then sew the 3½″ × 11″ Slate background piece to the top. Sew the 1½″ × 3″ Slate background piece to the bottom of the row from Step 7 of the Regatta/Celery block, and then sew the 6″ × 10″ Slate background piece to the left of the row. Sew this section to the bottom of the Aqua/Khaki block section.

3. Sew the 2½″ × 6½″ Slate background piece to the top of the row from Step 5 of the Regatta/Celery block. Sew this section to the left of the Ash/Lake block.

4. Sew the 3½″ × 6½″ Slate background piece to the right of the Regatta/Celery block, and then sew the 3″ × 9½″ Slate background piece to the bottom of the block.

5. Sew the Regatta/Celery block section to the bottom of the Ash/Lake block section. Sew this combined section to the right-hand side of the Aqua/Khaki block section.

6. Sew the 3″ × 5″ Slate background piece to the left side of the Green Tea/Light Parfait square row. Stitch the row to the bottom of the section formed in Step 5.

7. The section should now measure 20″ wide × 20½″ high.

Section D

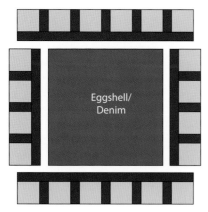

Section D assembly diagram

This section has 1 Eggshell/Denim block.

SECTION D CUTTING CHART

FABRIC	QUANTITY	SIZE
Slate (subcut from basic strips)	1	1½″ × 39″
	1	1½″ × 9″
	2	1½″ × 20½″
	2	1½″ × 13½″
Denim	1	13½″ × 13½″
Eggshell	1	3″ × 39″
	1	3″ × 9″
	4	3″ × 3″

Eggshell/Denim block

1. Stitch the 3″ × 39″ Eggshell strip to the 1½″ × 39″ Slate divider strip; press. Subcut into 13 pieces, 3″ wide. Stitch the 3″ × 9″ Eggshell strip to the 1½″ × 9″ Slate divider strip; press. Subcut into 3 pieces 3″ wide. You now have 16 identical pieces 3″ × 4″.

2. Stitch together 5 pieces from Step 1 plus a final Eggshell square 3″ × 3″ for the top row. Repeat for the bottom row. Stitch a 1½″ × 20½″ Slate divider strip to each row.

3. Stitch together 3 pieces plus a final Eggshell square 3″ × 3″ for the left row. Repeat for the right row. Stitch a 1½″ × 13½″ Slate divider strip to each row.

4. Stitch the rows from Step 3 to the left and right sides of the 13½″ × 13½″ Denim square. Stitch the rows from Step 2 to the top and bottom of the Denim block.

5. The section should now measure 20½″ × 20½″.

Section E

Section E assembly diagram

Section E has 1 Sage/Robin Egg block.

SECTION E CUTTING CHART

FABRIC	QUANTITY	SIZE
Slate (subcut from basic strips)	1	1″ × 30″
	2	1″ × 7½″
	3	1″ × 10½″
	1	1″ × 11″
Slate (cut from remaining fabric)	1	11″ × 10″
Robin Egg	1	7½″ × 7½″
Sage	1	1½″ × 30″
	4	1½″ × 1½″

Sage/Robin Egg block

1. Stitch the 1½″ × 30″ Sage strip to the 1″ × 30″ Slate divider strip; press. Subcut into 20 pieces 1½″ wide.

2. Stitch together 6 pieces from Step 1 plus a final Sage square 1½″ × 1½″ for the top row. Repeat for the bottom row. Stitch a 1″ × 10½″ Slate divider strip to each row.

3. Stitch together 4 pieces from Step 1 plus a final Sage square 1½″ × 1½″ for the left row. Repeat for the right row. Stitch a 1″ × 7½″ Slate divider strip to each row.

4. Stitch the rows from Step 3 to the left and right sides of the 7½″ × 7½″ Robin Egg square. Stitch the rows from Step 2 to the top and bottom of the block.

Section E assembly

1. Refer to the Section E assembly diagram (page 110). Sew a 1″ × 10½″ Slate background strip to the left side of the block. Sew the 1″ × 11″ Slate background strip to the top of the block. Sew the 11″ × 10″ Slate background piece to the bottom of the block.

2. The section should now measure 11″ × 20½″.

Section F

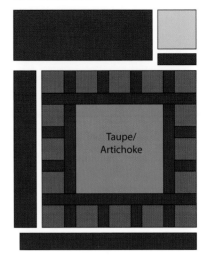

Section F assembly diagram

Section F has 1 Taupe/Artichoke block.

SECTION F CUTTING CHART

FABRIC	QUANTITY	SIZE
Slate (subcut from basic strips)	1	1½″ × 30″
	2	1½″ × 8½″
	2	1½″ × 14½″
	1	1½″ × 4″
Slate (cut from remaining fabric)	1	5″ × 13″
	1	2½″ × 14½″
	1	2″ × 16½″
Artichoke	1	8½″ × 8½″
Taupe	1	2½″ × 30″
	4	2½″ × 2½″
Green Tea	1	4″ × 4″

Taupe/Artichoke block

1. Stitch the 2½″ × 30″ Taupe strip to the 1½″ × 30″ Slate divider strip; press. Subcut into 12 pieces 2½″ wide.

2. Stitch together 4 pieces from Step 1 plus a final Taupe square 2½″ × 2½″ for the top row. Repeat for the bottom row. Stitch a 1½″ × 14½″ Slate divider strip to each row.

3. Stitch together 2 pieces plus a final Taupe square 2½″ × 2½″ for the left row. Repeat for the right row. Stitch a 1½″ × 8½″ Slate divider strip to each row.

4. Stitch the rows from Step 3 to the left and right side of the Artichoke square 8½″ × 8½″. Stitch the rows from Step 2 to the top and bottom of the block.

Section F assembly

1. Refer to the Section F assembly diagram (page 111) to sew the 2½″ × 14½″ Slate background piece to the left side of the block. Sew the 2″ × 16½″ Slate background piece to the bottom.

2. Sew the 1½″ × 4″ Slate divider strip to the bottom of the 4″ × 4″ Green Tea square. Sew the 5″ × 13″ Slate background piece to left side.

3. Sew the Green Tea section to the top of the Taupe/Artichoke section.

4. The section should now measure 16½″ × 20½″.

Section G

Section G assembly diagram

Section G has 1 Green Tea/Light Parfait partial block.

SECTION G CUTTING CHART

FABRIC	QUANTITY	SIZE
Slate (subcut from basic strips)	1	1½″ × 16″
	2	1½″ × 8½″
	1	1½″ × 14″
Slate (cut from remaining fabric)	1	8″ × 14″
Light Parfait	1	8½″ × 8½″
Green Tea	1	4″ × 16″
	1	4″ × 4″

Green Tea/Light Parfait partial block

1. Stitch the 4″ × 16″ Green Tea strip to the 1½″ × 16″ Slate divider strip; press. Subcut into 4 pieces 4″ wide.

2. Stitch together 3 pieces from Step 1 (with no final square) for the bottom. Position the row so that the Green Tea square is at the far right, and stitch the 1½″ × 14″ Slate divider strip to the top of the row.

3. Stitch 1 piece from Step 1 plus a final Green Tea square 4″ × 4″ for the right row. Stitch a 1½″ × 8½″ Slate divider strip to the row.

4. Stitch the row from Step 3 to the right-hand side of the 8½″ × 8½″ Light Parfait square. Stitch a 1½″ × 8½″ Slate divider strip to the left side of the square. Stitch the row from Step 2 to the bottom of the block.

Section G assembly

1. Refer to the Section G assembly diagram to sew the 8″ × 14″ Slate background piece to the bottom of the block.

2. The section should now measure 14″ × 20½″.

Quilt top assembly

1. Refer to the quilt assembly diagram (page 104) to arrange Sections A–G on a design wall or flat surface.

2. Sew Section A to Section B; press toward B.

3. Sew Section C to the right of Section A/B; press toward C.

4. Sew Section D to Section E; press toward E.

5. Sew Section F to Section G; press toward G.

6. Sew section D/E to Section F/G; press toward F/G.

7. Sew the top sections to the bottom sections. Press toward the top of the quilt.

8. The quilt top should now measure 60½˝ × 40½˝.

Quilting and finishing

1. Mark quilting designs on the quilt top or plan to stitch without marking.

2. Use your preferred method or refer to Quiltmaking Basics (page 135) to layer and baste the quilt top, batting, and backing.

3. Quilt by hand or machine. I quilted closely spaced lines on all sections. Within the squares, I quilted concentric squares, triangular quadrants, or simple rows.

4. Use your preferred method or refer to Quiltmaking Basics to bind the quilt.

SWEET AS PI
BABY QUILT

Designed and made by Malka Dubrawsky

Finished quilt size: 40½″ in diameter

Years ago I swam on a team whose coach, having created what could best be described as a convoluted workout, would proclaim, "It looks complicated, but it really isn't." The same could be said of this design. Despite its circular shape and the multiplicity of colored strips, this baby quilt is amazingly simple to piece and can be easily described as a weekend project.

The inspiration for this design came from two much-loved concepts—simple geometry and large scale. I've long been fascinated with making shaped quilts. Though I do recognize that squares and rectangles are shapes, I like the idea of quilts that come together to make shapes other than the standard. I'm also interested in the scale of the elements that make up a quilt. To that end, I enlarged the strips used in this design and crafted them out of a spectrum of colors to enhance and highlight the simplicity of the quilt. I further emphasized the energy of the quilt top by quilting it in concentric octagons radiating out from the center.

MATERIALS AND SUPPLIES

Cactus: ⅛ yard

Pistachio: ¼ yard

Coral: ½ yard

Peacock, Jade Green, Rich Red, and Bright Pink: ¾ yard of each

Salmon: 1⅛ yards

Cotton batting: 46″ × 46″

Banner paper: about 48″ × 48″*

String: 1 piece 20½″ long

This extra-large paper is available at office supply stores.

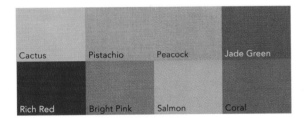

CUTTING

Cactus:
Cut 8 strips 3″ × 4″.

Pistachio:
Cut 8 strips 3″ × 5″.

Peacock:
Cut 8 strips 3″ × 7″.

Cut 1 square 23½″ × 23½″ for pieced backing.

Jade Green:
Cut 8 strips 3″ × 10″.

Cut 1 square 23½″ × 23½″ for pieced backing.

Rich Red:
Cut 8 strips 3″ × 12″.

Cut 1 square 23½″ × 23½″ for pieced backing.

Coral:
Cut 8 strips 3″ × 14″.

Bright Pink:
Cut 8 strips 3″ × 16″.

Cut 1 square 23½″ × 23½″ for pieced backing.

Salmon:
Cut 8 strips 4½″ × 18″.

Cut 2″ strips on the bias for 140″ of diagonally seamed binding strips.

INSTRUCTIONS

All seam allowances are ¼″. Unless otherwise indicated, press seams to one side, alternating sides where seams intersect.

NOTE

I like to make my designs adaptable for the user, and this one is no exception. Rather than create a template for you to trace or photocopy, I have included directions for making the pie-shaped wedge used as the template. Because you craft your own template, you can easily adapt the size of the finished quilt, if you wish, by altering the size of your template.

Creating the template

1. Fold the banner paper in half to create a center crease; fold in half again to create a second crease perpendicular to the first.

2. Open the folded paper to reveal 4 creased quadrants.

3. Lay the paper on a large, flat surface. Tape an end of the string to the center point on the paper and tape the other end to a pencil.

4. Carefully draw an arc between 2 creased lines in 1 quadrant.

5. Using paper scissors, cut out the quadrant with the drawn arc.

6. Fold the quadrant in half to reveal the midpoint of the arc, and cut the paper at the crease. The template created is a one-eighth wedge of a circle.

Wedge assembly

1. Fold 1 Cactus strip in half. Finger-press the crease and open the strip.

2. Repeat Step 1 with a Pistachio strip.

3. Pin the Cactus and Pistachio strips right sides together, aligning the long edges and center creases. Stitch a long edge and press.

4. Fold in half and finger-press a Peacock strip.

5. Pin the Peacock strip to the sewn Cactus/Pistachio pair of strips, right sides together, along the long edge. Stitch and press.

6. Continue creasing, pinning, sewing, and pressing strips as shown until the unit contains a strip of each color.

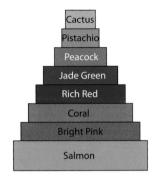

7. Position the template on top of the sewn strips, aligning the center of the arc with the creased center of the Salmon strip and the point of the wedge with the creased center of the Cactus strip. Pin to secure.

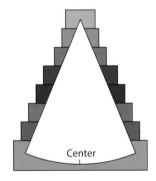

8. Using a rotary cutter, cut around the template, adding a ¼˝ seam allowance on all sides, to create a wedge shape.

9. Repeat Steps 1–8 to create 8 wedge pieces.

Quilt top assembly

NOTE

Accuracy is important. Place a pin at every seam.

1. Pin 2 wedge pieces, right sides together, matching the seams. Sew them together and press.

2. Repeat Step 1 to create a second sewn pair of wedges.

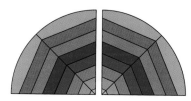

3. Pin the 2 sewn wedge pairs right sides together, matching the seams. Sew them together and press the seam open.

4. Repeat Steps 1–3 to sew together the remaining 4 wedges.

5. Pin the half-circle sections right sides together along their common straight edge, and then sew. Press the seam open.

Backing assembly

1. Pin the Jade Green and Rich Red squares right sides together. Sew them together along 1 side and press.

2. Repeat Step 1 with the Peacock and Bright Pink squares.

3. Pin the pairs of sewn squares, right sides together, along the common long edge, so that the colors are positioned as shown in the quilt back photo. Sew them together and press the seam open.

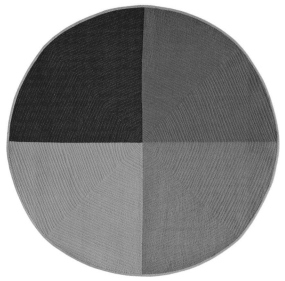

Quilt back

Quilting and finishing

1. Mark a quilting design on the quilt top, or plan to stitch without marking.

2. Use your favorite method or refer to Quiltmaking Basics (page 135) to layer and baste the quilt top, batting, and backing.

3. Quilt through the layers, removing the basting as you work. I chose to quilt in straight lines, forming concentric octagons radiating out from the center. Trim the edges of the batting and backing even with the quilt top.

4. Use your favorite method or refer to Quiltmaking Basics to join the binding strips with diagonal seams and bind the quilt.

THINK BIG

Designed and made by Jacquie Gering and quilted by Angela Walters

Finished quilt size: 57½″ × 75½″

On a visit to a local preschool I watched busy three- and four-year-olds build with giant blocks almost as big as they were. After building time was over, those colorful blocks were strewn over the floor of the playroom very much like the shapes in this quilt. Those industrious preschoolers inspired me to think big as I designed the quilt for this book.

Going large is one way to modernize a quilt design. Big blocks and bright colors make a bold statement in this quilt. Oversized shapes float on a color-blocked background to create a modern, minimalist design. I chose some of my favorite Kona Cotton Solids to showcase in this quilt. Some of the color combinations are high in contrast and pop from the background, while others are closer in value and recede. The value differences add interest and depth to the quilt. The quilting showcases the giant shapes as well as the color-blocked background.

Simple, graphic, and colorful are three of my favorite things in a quilt design. *Think Big* has them all.

MATERIALS AND SUPPLIES

Jade Green:

1¼ yards (Fabric A)

Snow: 1½ yards (Fabric B)

Lagoon: ¾ yard (Fabric C)

School Bus: ⅝ yard (Fabric D)

Cerise: 1¼ yards (Fabric E)

Chartreuse: ⅝ yard (Fabric F)

Curry: ⅜ yard (Fabric G)

Binding: ⅝ yard

Backing: 4 yards*

Low-loft cotton batting: 66″ × 84″

*Extra yardage may be required if backing fabric is less than 42″ wide.

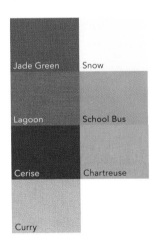

CUTTING

Label fabric pieces with their letter/number combination as you cut. This will allow you to lay out each panel quickly and easily. Cut the width-of-fabric (WOF) strips, and then subcut the pieces from those.

Jade Green (Fabric A):
Cut 1 strip 9½″ × WOF; subcut into these pieces:

   A1: 9½″ × 15½″

   A5: 6½″ × 6½″

   A6: 5″ × 9½″

   A7: 9½″ × 6½″

Cut 1 strip 3½″ × WOF; subcut into this piece:

   A3: 3½″ × 21½″

Cut 1 strip 24½″ × WOF; subcut into these pieces:

   A2: 11″ × 24½″

   A4: 15½″ × 21½″

Snow (Fabric B):
Cut 3 strips 5″ × WOF; subcut into these pieces:

   B2: 5″ × 18½″

   B5: 5″ × 15½″

   B6: 5″ × 24½″

   B9: 5″ × 15½″

   B10: 5″ × 21½″

   B13: 5″ × 14″

Snow (Fabric B), continued:
Cut 2 strips 6½″ × WOF; subcut into these pieces:

   B1: 6½″ × 9½″

   B3: 6½″ × 18½″

   B4: 6½″ × 21½″

   B7: 3½″ × 15½″

Cut 1 strip 9½″ × WOF; subcut into this piece:

   B8: 9½″ × 15½″

Cut 1 strip 8″ × WOF; subcut into these pieces:

   B11: 8″ × 21½″

   B12: 8″ × 8″

Lagoon (Fabric C):
Cut 1 strip 15½″ × WOF; subcut into these pieces:

   C1: 2″ × 15½″

   C2: 3½″ × 11″

   C3: 6½″ × 11″

   C4: 6½″ × 15½″

   C5: 3½″ × 11″

   C6: 6½″ × 11″

Cut 1 strip 6½″ × WOF; subcut into these pieces:

   C7: 3½″ × 12½″

   C8: 6½″ × 8″

   C9: 5″ × 12½″

Cutting, continued

School Bus (Fabric D):

Cut 1 strip 15½″ × WOF; subcut into these pieces:

  D1: 3½″ × 11″

  D2: 9½″ × 11″

  D3: 2″ × 15½″

  D4: 3½″ × 15½″

Cerise (Fabric E):

Cut 1 strip 15½″ × WOF; subcut into these pieces:

  E1: 15½″ × 27½″

  E5: 3½″ × 12½″

Cut 1 strip 5″ × WOF; subcut into this piece:

  E3: 5″ × 23″

Cut 1 strip 8″ × WOF; subcut into these pieces:

  E2: 8″ × 21½″

  E6: 6½″ × 8″

Cut 1 strip 12½″ × WOF; subcut into these pieces:

  E4: 5″ × 21½″

  E7: 12½″ × 18½″

Chartreuse (Fabric F):

Cut 1 piece F1: 6½″ × 17″.

Cut 1 piece F2: 8″ × 29″.

Cut 1 piece F3: 2″ × 29″.

Cut 1 piece F4: 2″ × 17″.

Curry (Fabric G):

Cut 1 piece G2: 2″ × 15½″.

Cut 1 strip 6½″ × WOF; subcut into these pieces:

  G1: 5″ × 15½″

  G3: 6½″ × 11

Binding:

Cut 8 strips 2¼″ × WOF for double-fold binding.

INSTRUCTIONS

All seam allowances are ¼″. Press seams open unless otherwise indicated.

This quilt lacks the regular block structure of a traditional quilt; instead, it is made up of 6 panels of various sizes, which are constructed individually and then put together to form the quilt top.

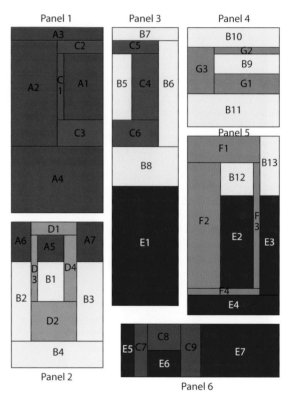

Quilt assembly diagram

Panel assembly

1. Refer to the quilt assembly diagram to lay out the labeled pieces in the correct positions to form Panels 1–6.

2. To make Panel 1, sew A1 to C1; then sew on the remaining pieces in the following order: C3, C2, A2, A3, A4.

3. To make Panel 2, sew B2 to A6 and B3 to A7. Place these sections back in the correct positions in Panel 2. Sew B1 to A5; then sew on the remaining pieces in the following order: D4, D3, D1, D2, A6/B2, A7/B3, B4.

4. To make Panel 3, sew C4 to B5; then sew on the remaining pieces in the following order: C5, C6, B6, B7, B8, E1.

5. To make Panel 4, sew G2 to B9; then sew on the remaining pieces in the following order: G1, G3, B10, B11.

6. To make Panel 5, sew E3 to B13. Place this section back in the correct position in Panel 5. Sew B12 to E2; then sew on the remaining pieces in the following order: F2, F3, F1, F4, E3/B13, E4.

7. To make Panel 6, sew C8 to E6; then sew on the remaining pieces in the following order: C7, E5, C9, E7.

Quilt top assembly

As you assemble the panels, be sure to match seams carefully so that the colors line up across the panels. Press as you go.

1. Sew Panel 2 to the bottom of Panel 1.

2. Sew Panel 5 to the bottom of Panel 4.

3. Sew Panel 3 and Panel 4/5 together.

4. Sew Panel 6 to the bottom of the section formed in Step 3.

5. Sew Panel 1/2 to the left side of the section formed in Step 4. Press the assembled quilt top.

Quilting and finishing

Have some fun on the back of the quilt with any leftover fabrics.

1. Mark quilting designs on the quilt top or plan to stitch without marking.

2. Use your favorite method or refer to Quiltmaking Basics (page 135) to layer and baste the quilt top, batting, and backing.

3. Quilt as desired by hand or machine. I chose to machine quilt, unifying the shapes with identical concentric straight-line quilting. Each background color is filled with a different curved quilting design, adding a bit of whimsy to this simple quilt.

4. Use your favorite method or refer to Quiltmaking Basics to sew together the 8 binding strips and bind the quilt.

TV COLOR BARS QUILT WITH PILLOW POCKET

Designed and made by Betz White

Finished quilt size: 70½″ × 54½″

This quilt is the perfect throw to snuggle under in front of the tube. In pillow form, it stays neatly folded up on your couch, disguised as a black-and-white TV with lousy reception. When the popcorn's ready and the movie begins, open it up into a bright and bold blanket of Technicolor.

The quilt's graphic design is based on the SMPTE color bars—a type of television test pattern developed in the 1970s used to correct video signals. Growing up with network TV (before cable, DVDs, and the Internet!), this was a familiar image to me when channels went off the air. In quilt form, the video rainbow is bold and modern, while evoking a sense of nostalgia and simplicity. Zigzags of "static" run across the TV pillow screen in graphic black and white.

MATERIALS AND SUPPLIES

(FOR QUILT AND PILLOW)

Medium Grey, Corn Yellow, Lagoon, Chartreuse, Bright Pink, Tomato, Ocean: ⅓ yard each*

Nightfall, White, Mulberry: ⅜ yard each

Slate: 1⅛ yard

Black for quilt top and pillow, including binding: 2⅛ yards

Backing for quilt: 3¾ yards

Batting for quilt: 63″ × 79″

Batting for pillow: 20″ × 20″

Buttons: 3 or 4, assorted sizes, for TV knobs

Chalk marker

Spray starch

Kona Cotton Solids used in this project are 44″ wide. If using a narrower fabric, you may need more yardage.

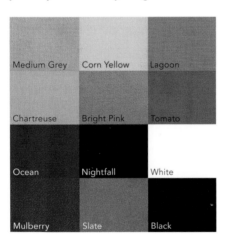

CUTTING

FOR THE QUILT:

Medium Grey, Corn Yellow, Lagoon, Chartreuse, Bright Pink, Tomato, and Ocean:
Cut 1 rectangle 10½″ × 35½″ from each for the large color bars.

Ocean, Bright Pink, Lagoon, and Medium Grey:
Cut 1 rectangle 10½″ × 5½″ from each for the small color bars.

Black:
Cut 3 rectangles 10½″ × 5½″ for the small color bars.

Cut 1 square 14½″ × 14½″ for the color squares.

Cut and piece a bias strip 2½″ × 260″ for double-fold binding.

Nightfall, White, Mulberry, and Slate:
Cut 1 square 14½″ × 14½″ from each for the color squares.

FOR THE PILLOW:

Slate:
Cut 2 squares 20″ × 20″ for the pillow top and back.

White:
Cut 1 rectangle 12½″ × 16″ for the "TV screen."

Black:
Cut 3 rectangles 4″ × 16″ for the zigzags.

Cut and piece a bias strip 2½″ × 58″ for double-fold binding.

Quilt

Quilt folded to form pillow

NOTE

Kaufman Kona Cotton Solids have no "right" and "wrong" side because they are piece-dyed. To clarify, yarn-dyed means the yarn is dyed first, then woven into fabric. This technique allows for the creation of multicolored patterns, such as plaid or woven stripe or gingham. Piece-dyed fabric is woven using undyed yarns, then the whole fabric is dyed at once.

INSTRUCTIONS

All seam allowances are ¼˝.

Pillow top assembly

1. To create "static" zigzags, place 1 Black 4˝ × 16˝ rectangle right side down (see Note, page 129) on your work surface. Using a chalk marker, draw a center line down the length of the rectangle 2˝ from each edge. Next, measure and mark perpendicular lines between the center line and an edge, every 2˝, alternating sides. With scissors, cut each marked perpendicular line from edge to center line.

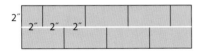

2. Using a hot iron, fold the first cut to the outside edge and press, creating a triangle. Repeat, folding in triangles, carefully matching points, and pressing. Continue until a zigzag is created. Spray lightly with starch.

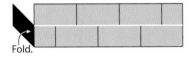

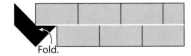

3. Repeat Steps 1 and 2 with the other 2 Black 4˝ × 16˝ rectangles to create a total of 3 zigzags.

4. Arrange the zigzags horizontally, right side up, on the right side of the White 12½˝ × 16˝ rectangle. Pin to secure, and topstitch the zigzags to the "screen."

5. Round the corners of the screen by tracing the curve of a bowl (about 4½˝ in diameter) and trimming along the marked line. Press under one short end of the 2½˝ × 58˝ Black bias strip ¼˝ to the wrong side. Press the strip in half lengthwise with wrong sides together to make a double-fold binding. Sew it to the back of the screen, overlapping the unfolded end with the beginning fold. Then flip the binding to the front and topstitch the edge of the binding.

6. Place the screen, with binding face up, onto the right side of the Slate 20˝ × 20˝ pillow top, about 3˝ down from the top edge, 5˝ up from the bottom edge, and about 2˝ from either side. Place the Slate pillow top and back right sides together, place the pillow batting on top, and pin the layers together. Sew the side and top seams, leaving the bottom edge open. Turn right side out, pushing out the corners and edges.

7. Baste the pillow top using your preferred method, such as curved safety pins.

8. Echo quilt on the white areas, about ¼″ from the edge of the black zigzags.

9. Hand sew buttons for TV knobs. Topstitch ¼″ from the bottom edge of the pillow top to secure the layers, and close the opening.

Quilt top assembly

1. Refer to the quilt assembly diagram to sew the large color bars to the small color bars in the order shown. Then sew the large/small sewn color bars together, side by side, as shown.

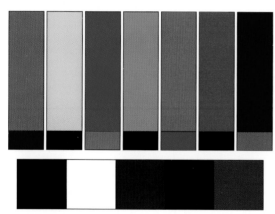

Quilt assembly diagram

2. Sew the color squares together, side by side, as shown. Sew the assembled squares to the assembled bars.

3. True up the quilt top by trimming the edges and making sure they are square.

Quilting and finishing

1. Layer the backing, batting, and quilt top. The batting and backing will be 4″ bigger all the way around the quilt top. Baste the quilt using your preferred method, such as curved safety pins.

2. Apply masking tape in vertical stripes (following the direction of the color bars), every 3″. Starting with the center and working outward, machine quilt, aligning the walking foot with the edge of each tape strip. You may choose to match thread colors, or use black on the dark colors and white on the lighter colors, or use a single thread color for all of the quilting.

3. Trim the excess batting and backing so that the quilt measures 54½″ × 70½″. Using an 8″–9″ plate and a chalk tool, mark rounded corners and trim. Topstitch the perimeter of the quilt about ⅛″ from the edge.

4. On the back of the quilt, pin the pillow top face down, centered on a short edge of the quilt. The bottom edge of the pillow should be aligned with the edge of the quilt.

5. Bind the quilt using your preferred method or referring to Quiltmaking Basics (page 135). Make sure to catch the bottom edge of the pillow top in the binding.

6. Hand stitch the sides of the pillow to the back of the quilt using a blind stitch. Leave the top of the pillow pocket open.

FOLDING INSTRUCTIONS

1. Place the quilt on a flat surface with the pillow side down. Fold the quilt lengthwise into thirds. Flip the quilt over.

2. Turn the pillow portion right side out by reaching inside and grasping the corners.

3. Fold the quilt into fourths. At the last fold, insert the quilt into the pillow and pat smooth.

INTERVIEW
with Denyse Schmidt

In her glorious improvisational quilts, Denyse Schmidt makes use of solid fabrics and colors in fresh and unique ways. She spoke with Susanne Woods about her own special Paper Bag Piecing technique, which she uses with great success to help her students choose and combine colors to create their own one-of-a-kind quilts.

SW: Tell me how your Paper Bag Piecing technique works.

DS: I devised my Paper Bag Piecing technique for my students, as a way to facilitate the process of creating improvisational patchwork. Improvisation in any form—whether music, dance, or patchwork—is about being in the moment and responding to what is happening now, rather than creating strictly according to preconceived ideas.

This doesn't mean that there isn't a foundation of skill, or even an underlying structure. Good structure is in fact essential to the process. In patchwork, the nature of the materials, as well as the fact that you can only sew one piece to another at a time, provides at least part of an inherent structure or system.

But for the students in my workshops, the intuitive part of choosing which color to use next or how to put it all together seemed to be the sticking point. When I started teaching in 2002, most quilting instruction involved exacting standards such as precision point matching, as well as very well-defined rules about choosing colors and fabrics. For many of today's sewists—especially aspiring quilters—these requirements can seem intimidating. Also, because we tend to buy fabrics we are drawn to, we often end up with a

stash of fabrics in a limited range of value, hue or print scale. Then we can't understand why our quilts always look the same, no matter how hard we try to try create something different.

I think that my Paper Bag technique is successful because it's so simple. For my workshops, I fill three paper bags with random pieces or scraps of fabric sorted by relative size. The fabrics are a riot of colors, values, patterns, and solids. Without looking, everyone draws one piece at a time out of the bag. The idea is to use each piece in the order drawn, as is. The process is fun because it removes the burden of choosing colors and shapes or deciding between prints and solids for each piece you will add to a block. The process moves along quickly, which is also rewarding.

Once you can give yourself over to the process, it's incredibly freeing. At some point in the workshop, every student will sew together two fabrics they would normally never put anywhere near each other, only to discover a magic in the combination that makes the block come alive. For many of us, it's scary to let go and invest time in something without being able to guarantee "good" (familiar) results. But my theory is that real learning comes when we are willing to take risks and step outside of what we are comfortable with.

Wendy's Dresses, 85″×91″, designed and made by Denyse Schmidt, using a little girl's dresses; hand quilted by Amish women in Minnesota

SW: How much do you control the color palette of the fabric

DS: Before every workshop, I replenish the bags with scraps from my bins, as well as fabrics I cut for the purpose. I'm in total control of what goes in the bags in terms of color and whether it's a print or a solid. What I don't control, however, is what comes out of the bag, and when. It's pure, random chance, and it's always amazing—and unpredictable—to see how things play out. Some people suspect the bags on another table have more prints than the bags they are using, and they switch bags only to find the "solid karma" is theirs alone!

SW: What is it about the improvisational style that you think has been so appealing to a new generation of sewists?

DS: An improvisational style appeals to the new generation for a couple of reasons. Inherent in the process is the idea that it's okay to make mistakes. This is something that appealed to me in the antique, utilitarian, and African-American quilts that first inspired my own work. These quilts, with their little quirks and charming imperfections, come alive because of this evidence of the maker's unique personality and humanness. The idea that a quilt can be made without having to learn a lot of rules or achieve perfect sewing skills is appealing because in today's world, not everyone has the time to devote to an exacting craft. Quilts require big investments of time, but an improvised patchwork top can often go together much faster than one using traditional patchwork patterns. The process can also be more engaging and intuitive, more akin to making a collage or a painting, than the typical stages of cutting and sewing a traditional quilt.

SW: How do color and the use of solids play into this style?

DS: While color and solids can be used to wonderful effect in any style of patchwork, the improvisational style easily allows for wonderful, surprising combinations of colors. Of course, a quilter can apply those same unexpected color combinations to a traditional pattern, but sometimes a more free-form patchwork approach lends itself more to exploration and experimentation.

SW: In your own work, when do you make the decision to use a solid as opposed to a print or a print that reads as a solid?

DS: When I started my business in 1996, one thing I identified in early quilts that seemed to be missing in contemporary work was the more liberal use of solids and of tiny calicos and prints that read like solids. Much of the contemporary work at the time utilized the cornucopia of printed quilting fabrics available, which is understandable. But the simplicity of the earlier quilts appealed to me more, so I tended to use a larger percentage of solids than prints in my work. There was also a practical reason for using more solids. Print collections come and go, but solid collections are generally available from year to year. This meant I'd be able to replicate quilt designs for my clients over time without having to find suitable substitutes for prints no longer available. I continue to use a larger percentage of solids in my work for the same reasons.

Photo by Frank Poole
Run & Fall, 85″ × 91″, designed and made by Denyse Schmidt; hand quilted by Amish women in Minnesota

QUILTMAKING BASICS
HOW TO FINISH A QUILT

General Guidelines

SEAM ALLOWANCES

A ¼″ seam allowance is used for most projects. It's a good idea to do a test seam before you begin sewing to check that your ¼″ is accurate. Accuracy is the key to successful piecing.

There is no need to backstitch unless stated in the project instructions. Usually seamlines will be crossed by another seam, which will anchor the stitches.

PRESSING

In general, press seams toward the darker fabric. Press lightly in an up-and-down motion. Avoid using a very hot iron or overironing, which can distort shapes and blocks. Be especially careful when pressing bias edges because they stretch easily.

Backing

Plan on making the backing a minimum of 8″ longer and wider than the quilt top. Piece, if necessary. Trim the selvages before you piece to the desired size.

To economize, piece the back from any leftover quilting fabrics or blocks in your collection.

Batting

The type of batting to use is a personal decision; consult your local quilt shop. Cut batting approximately 8″ longer and wider than your quilt top. Note that your batting choice will affect how much quilting is necessary for the quilt. Check the manufacturer's instructions to see how far apart the quilting lines can be.

Layering

Spread the backing wrong side up and tape the edges down with masking tape. (If you are working on carpet you can use T-pins to secure the backing to the carpet.) Center the batting on top, smoothing out any folds. Place the quilt top right side up on top of the batting and backing, making sure it is centered.

Basting

Basting keeps the quilt "sandwich" layers from shifting while you are quilting.

If you plan to machine quilt, pin baste the quilt layers together with safety pins placed about 3″–4″ apart. Begin basting in the center and move toward the edges first in vertical, then horizontal, rows. Try not to pin directly on the intended quilting lines.

If you plan to hand quilt, baste the layers together with thread using a long needle and light-colored thread. Knot an end of the thread. Using stitches approximately the length of the needle, begin in the center and move out toward the edges in vertical and horizontal rows approximately 4″ apart. Then add 2 diagonal rows of basting.

Quilting

Quilting, whether by hand or machine, enhances the pieced or appliquéd design of the quilt. You may choose to quilt in-the-ditch, echo the pieced or appliqué motifs, use patterns from quilting design books and stencils, or do your own free-motion quilting. Remember to check your batting manufacturer's recommendations for how close the quilting lines must be.

Binding

Trim excess batting and backing from the quilt, even with the edges of the quilt top.

DOUBLE-FOLD STRAIGHT-GRAIN BINDING

For a ¼″ finished binding, cut the binding strips 2″ wide and piece them together with diagonal seams to make a continuous binding strip. Trim the seam allowance to ¼″. Press the seams open.

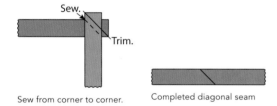

Sew from corner to corner.   Completed diagonal seam

Press the entire strip in half lengthwise with wrong sides together. With raw edges even, pin the binding to the front edge of the quilt a few inches away from a corner, and leave the first few inches of the binding unattached. Start sewing (through both layers of binding, the quilt top, the batting, and the backing), using a ¼″ seam allowance.

Stop ¼″ away from the first corner you come to (see Step 1), and backstitch 1 stitch. Lift the presser foot and needle. Rotate the quilt a quarter turn. Fold the binding at a right angle

so it extends straight above the quilt and the fold forms a 45° angle in the corner (see Step 2). Then bring the binding strip down even with the edge of the quilt (see Step 3). Begin sewing at the folded edge. Repeat in the same manner at all corners.

Continue stitching until you are back near the beginning of the binding strip. See Finishing the

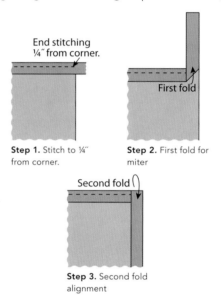

Step 1. Stitch to ¼″ from corner.

Step 2. First fold for miter

Step 3. Second fold alignment

Binding Ends (page 137) for tips on finishing and hiding the raw edges of the ends of the binding.

CONTINUOUS BIAS BINDING

A continuous bias involves using a square sliced in half diagonally and then sewing the triangles together so that you continuously cut marked strips to make continuous bias binding. The same instructions can be used to cut bias for piping. Cut the fabric for the bias binding or piping so it is a square. For example, if the yardage is ½ yard, cut an 18″ × 18″ square. Cut the square in half diagonally, creating 2 triangles.

Sew these triangles together as shown, using a ¼″ seam allowance. Press the seam open.

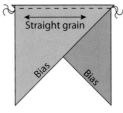

Sew triangles together.

Using a ruler, mark the parallelogram created by the two triangles with lines spaced the width you need to cut your bias. Cut about 5″ along the first line.

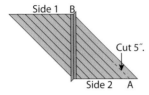

Mark lines and begin to cut.

Join Side 1 and Side 2 to form a tube. The raw edge at point A will align with the raw edge at B. This will allow the first line to be offset by the width of a strip. Pin the raw edges right sides together, making sure that the drawn lines match. Sew with a ¼″ seam allowance. Press the seam open. Cut along the drawn lines, creating a single continuous strip.

Press the entire strip in half lengthwise with wrong sides together. Place binding on the quilt as described in Double-Fold Straight-Grain Binding (page 136).

FINISHING THE BINDING ENDS

METHOD 1

After stitching around the quilt, fold under the beginning tail of the binding strip ¼″ so that the raw edge will be inside the binding after it is turned to the back of the quilt. Place the end tail of the binding strip over the beginning folded end. Continue to attach the binding and stitch slightly beyond the starting stitches. Trim the excess binding. Fold the

binding over the raw edges to the quilt back and hand stitch, mitering the corners.

METHOD 2

See C&T Publishing's blog entry at ctpubblog.com, search for "invisible seam," then scroll down to "Quilting Tips: Completing a Binding with an Invisible Seam."

Fold the ending tail of the binding back on itself where it meets the beginning binding tail. From the fold, measure and mark the cut width of your binding strip. Cut the ending binding tail to this measurement. For example, if your binding is cut 2⅛″ wide, measure from the fold on the ending tail of the binding 2⅛″ and cut the binding tail to this length.

Cut binding tail.

Open both tails. Place a tail on top of the other tail at right angles, right sides together. Mark a diagonal line from corner to corner and stitch on the line. Check that you've done it correctly and that the binding fits the quilt; then trim the seam allowance to ¼″. Press open.

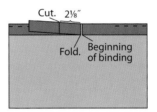

Stitch ends of binding diagonally.

Refold the binding and stitch this binding section in place on the quilt. Fold the binding over the raw edges to the quilt back and hand stitch.

ABOUT THE DESIGNERS

Photo by Marcia Ward/ImageMaker

LISA CALL

lisacall.com

Lisa is a visual artist who creates abstract contemporary textile paintings composed of her richly colored hand-dyed fabric. Her award-winning artwork is exhibited and published internationally and is included in numerous private and public collections. Lisa writes about her artwork, her processes, and her life as an artist on her blog. Lisa is the creator and author of MakeBigArt.com, devoted to empowering artists to think big about their art, their marketing, and their lives.

Photo by Gavin Carlton

ALISSA HAIGHT CARLTON

handmadebyalissa.com

Alissa has been obsessively quilting for five years. She is one of the founders of the Modern Quilt Guild as well as an author. She co-authored *Block Party—The Modern Quilting Bee* (Stash Books, an imprint of C&T Publishing), with Kristen Lejnieks; her most recent book is *Modern Minimal* (Stash Books, an imprint of C&T Publishing). When not quilting, Alissa casts TV reality shows, including seasons seven and eight of *Project Runway*.

Photo by Sean Cier

EMILY CIER
carolinapatchworks.com

Emily, creator of Carolina Patchworks, has had a lifelong love of fine art and art history and a background in graphic design. These passions have found a common ground in quilting. Emily makes abstract modern quilts. As Emily has rooted out the science in this art—or the art in this math—she's also discovered how to make these "pixel quilts" easy to construct, or at least no more difficult than a 500-piece puzzle (if those pieces came with an assembly diagram)! Emily is the author of *Quilt Remix, Scrap Republic,* and the forthcoming *Pixel Play* (C&T Publishing).

Photo by Alex and Eryn Chandler

MALKA DUBRAWSKY
stitchindye.com

Malka worked for several years primarily as a fiber artist. She was lucky enough to be included in some prestigious exhibitions such as Quilt National and Visions Art Museum, and publications such as *Fiberarts Design Book 7.* Recently she's been busy making more functional textiles, using primarily her own hand-dyed and patterned fabric. Her quilts and other creations are sold at stitchindye.etsy.com. Malka's patterns have appeared in numerous magazines and books. She is the author of *Color Your Cloth: A Quilter's Guide to Dyeing and Patterning Fabric* and *Fresh Quilting: Fearless, Color, Design, and Inspiration.* Read more about her work at stitchindye.blogspot.com.

Photo by Joseph Ellis

AMY ELLIS
www.amyscreativeside.com

Amy has loved fabric and sewing since she started sewing as a girl, making garments for herself. Later, as a wife and mother, making quilts was a natural progression. Quilting is Amy's creative therapy in the midst of a busy household, and she loves to share this passion with anyone who will listen! Amy is the author of *Modern Basics: Easy Quilts to Fit Your Budget, Space, and Style.* Many of Amy's quilts are simple yet interesting, making them a great starting point for anyone who wants to begin quilting.

Photo by Jim White Photography

MODERN QUILT STUDIOS
WEEKS RINGLE AND BILL KERR
modernquiltstudio.com

Weeks and Bill are founders of Modern Quilt Studio, a contemporary quilt and textile design studio. Their work is seen widely in the press, including in *O, the Oprah Magazine*; *Country Living*; *The New York Times*; *Quilts Japan*; *Time* magazine, *American Patchwork & Quilting*, and *Quilts and More* magazines. They are the authors of many books, including *The Modern Quilt Workshop*. Their most recent books are *Quilts Made Modern* and *Transparency Quilts* (C&T Publishing).

Photo by Jacquie Gering

JACQUIE GERING
tallgrassprairiestudio.blogspot.com

Jacquie designs and makes modern, improvisational quilts and is the co-author of *Quilting Modern: Techniques and Projects for Improvisational Quilts*. She is a contributing designer for *Stitch* and *Quilter's Home* magazines, a contributing author for *Quilter's World* magazine, and one of the designers featured in the book *Block Party—The Modern Quilting Bee*. Jacquie serves on the board of directors of the national Modern Quilt Guild, and is a founding member of the Kansas City Modern Quilt Guild. Jacquie shares her designs and quilting knowledge on her popular blog.

Photo by Jen Carlton Bailly

ELIZABETH HARTMAN
ohfransson.com

Elizabeth is a self-taught quiltmaker and pattern designer for modern sewing and quilting. Having grown up in a family that was always making things, she got hooked on quilting as soon as she tried it. She loves the play of color and pattern, the orderliness of the process, and perhaps best of all, the reward at the end—a fantastic and functional piece. Elizabeth is the author of *The Practical Guide to Patchwork* and *Modern Patchwork* (Stash Books, an imprint of C&T Publishing).

RITA HODGE
RED PEPPER QUILTS
www.redpepperquilts.com

Rita loves to make quilts and collect fabrics. Her quilting style is fresh and modern; she makes use of simple and often traditional design ideas. Rita has been both surprised and overwhelmed by the positive response to her blog, which is a journal of her creative self. She hopes to show readers that easy-to-make quilts can be really striking, especially if they take small risks in fabric and color selection.

Photo by Ashlee House

CHERRI HOUSE
cherryhousequilts.com

Cherri is a quilt designer and owner of Cherry House Quilts. Geometric and graphic quilts designed as a whole are Cherri's signature style. A constant in her quilting adventures is her love of color and fabric—"the more the merrier" is her motto. She is the author of *City Quilts* (Stash Books, an imprint of C&T Publishing). Cherri's first love has always been her family. Quilting often took a back seat while she was raising her children, but once they grew up, Cherry House Quilts was born—and a long-awaited dream came true!

Photo by Caitlin Harlan

KATHY MACK
pinkchalkstudio.com

Kathy's grandmother taught her to sew as a little girl, and she loves it as much today as she did after taking that first stitch. Pink Chalk Studio is her sewing pattern design company, where she adds color and artful design to things used every day. Kathy is also the proprietor of Pink Chalk Fabrics, an online fabric shop at PinkChalkFabrics.com.

JENNIFER SAMPOU
facebook.com/pages/Jennifer-Sampou/190180167716384

Jennifer studied textiles and surface design at the Fashion Institute of Technology in New York City and worked at Laura Ashley in Wales. She was creative director for P&B Textiles before opening Studio Sampou, where she created best-selling fabrics for Northcott Monarch Fabrics and Robert Kaufman Fabrics. With her sister, Carolyn Schmitz, she co-authored *In the Nursery* (C&T Publishing). Currently under exclusive fabric license to Robert Kaufman, Jennifer's fabrics can be seen at robertkaufman.com. Colorful *Fiesta* is her newest fabric line.

Photo by Lane duPont

DENYSE SCHMIDT
dsquilts.com

Denyse Schmidt is a quilter known for blending the traditional and modern, resulting in quilts that are offbeat yet sparse and sophisticated. She is also an author (*Denyse Schmidt Quilts: 30 Colorful Quilt and Patchwork Projects*), teacher, and quilt pattern designer. Her vintage-inspired fabric collections are produced by FreeSpirit Fabrics.

Photo by Ross Chandler

JEAN WELLS
jeanwellsquilts.com

An author, teacher, and owner of The Stitchin' Post quilt shop in Sisters, Oregon, Jean has written more than 28 books. Her most recent book, *Intuitive Color and Design* (C&T Publishing), features quilts made in the same style as her quilt in this book. In 1975, she started the world-famous Sisters Outdoor Quilt Show. Jean has won numerous awards and was also the first independent retailer to be inducted into the Primedia Hall of Fame. In 2010, she was inducted into the Quilters Hall of Fame as the 40th honoree.

VALORI WELLS
valoriwells.com

Valori is a professional quilter, fabric designer, author, and pattern designer. She is co-owner with her mother, Jean Wells, of The Stitchin' Post quilt shop in Sisters, Oregon. Valori's background in photography has contributed to her career as a fabric designer. As a quilter, she is always designing quilts in her mind as she paints her fabric designs. As an author, she has written *Simple Start, Stunning Finish* (C&T Publishing) as well as other books.

Photo by David White

BETZ WHITE
BetzWhite.com

Betz has built a career on thoughtful design, skilled craftsmanship, and a focus on materials that are kind to people and the planet alike. She is a designer, a green crafter, and author of *Warm Fuzzies* and *Sewing Green*. Her original sewing patterns, Make New or Make Do™, are designed to be made from either new or repurposed fabrics and are sold in specialty fabric shops nationwide. As an earth-friendly complement to her pattern line, Betz is thrilled to be partnering with Robert Kaufman to offer Stitch, a coordinated quilt collection of organic cotton sheeting.

Photo by Katja Kuorinki-Väänänen

KAJSA WIKMAN
syko.fi

Kajsa lives and works in Helsinki, Finland, as a full-time textile artist with her little business Syko. She specializes in playful and happy appliqué designs, and her products range from quilts and softies to pattern kits and printed postcards. Kajsa is the author of *Scandinavian Stitches* (Stash Books, an imprint of C&T Publishing). In her book, she chose to describe her attitude toward making happy art for everyday life as follows: Art can be playful and happy, and what could be more important than finding the simple joys in life?"

Resources

Shown here is a list of all the Kaufman Kona Cotton Solids featured in this book.*

1479 Amber	1004 Apricot	1005 Aqua	347 Artichoke	1007 Ash	348 Asparagus	1009 Azure	189 Baby Pink
1011 Bahama Blue	1481 Banana	1019 Black	1287PFD Bleach White	1028 Blue	1029 Blue Bell	277 Blueberry	1037 Bone
1042 Brick	1049 Bright Pink	1054 Burgundy	1055 Butter	1056 Buttercup	349 Butterscotch	199 Cactus	1058 Cadet
26 Canary	1060 Candy Blue	1061 Candy Green	1062 Candy Pink	1064 Caribbean	141 Carnation	355 Cayenne	1706 Celery
1066 Cerise	1069 Champagne	1071 Charcoal	1072 Chartreuse	350 Cheddar	152 Cloud	135 Clover	1080 Coal
1084 Copen	1087 Coral	1089 Corn Yellow	1090 Cream	142 Crocus	1677 Curry	1101 Delft Blue	1452 Denim
1465 Dusty Peach	138 Earth	1133 Eggplant	184 Eggshell	195 Evening	1144 Flesh	1703 Grass Green	351 Green Tea
340 Herb	188 Hibiscus	1162 Honey	21 Honey Dew	1161 Holly	1171 Hyacinth	1173 Ice Frappe	1176 Ice Peach
1178 Indigo	1181 Ivory	1183 Jade Green	147 Jungle	1185 Kelly	1187 Khaki	1188 Kiwi	139 Lagoon

194 Lake	357 Lapis	23 Lemon	1205 Light Parfait	1191 Lilac	1192 Lime	1484 Lupine	1215 Mahogany
1216 Maize	1223 Medium Grey	1225 Medium Pink	1229 Meringue	1234 Mint	1237 Mocha	80 Mulberry	1240 Mustard
1242 Natural	1243 Navy	140 Nightfall	25 Ocean	1263 Olive	1265 Orange	1271 Pale Flesh	149 Papaya
150 Paprika	198 Parsley	1281 Peach	1282 Peacock	145 Pear	1283 Pearl Pink	110 Peony	359 Pepper
317 Peridot	1285 Periwinkle	143 Petal	24 Petunia	1291 Pink	1293 Pistachio	1295 Pomegranate	274 Primrose
1306 Raffia	346 Regatta	1551 Rich Red	1514 Robin Egg	1321 Sage	1483 Salmon	1323 Sand	1482 School Bus
1328 Seafoam	1513 Sky	1336 Slate	1339 Snow	144 Sour Apple	159 Spice	1361 Spruce	1362 Stone
186 Straw	353 Sunflower	1369 Tan	1370 Tangerine	316 Tarragon	1371 Taupe	134 Thistle	7 Tomato
1383 Violet	1386 Wheat	1387 White	1388 Willow	1389 Windsor	1390 Wine	1478 Yarrow	354 Zucchini

Go to robertkaufman.com for the entire available palette of Kona Cotton Solids and a list of retail stores in your area.

stashBOOKS®

fabric arts for a handmade lifestyle

If you're craving beautiful authenticity in a time of mass-production...Stash Books is for you. Stash Books is a line of how-to books celebrating fabric arts for a handmade lifestyle. Backed by C&T Publishing's solid reputation for quality, Stash Books will inspire you with contemporary designs, clear and simple instructions, and engaging photography.

www.stashbooks.com